Greenhill Books

THROUGH THE
ZULU COUNTRY

Through the
ZULU COUNTRY
Its Battlefields and People

by Bertram Mitford

With an Introduction by Ian Knight

Greenhill Books, London
Presidio Press, California

This edition of *Through the Zulu Country* first published 1992
by Greenhill Books, Lionel Leventhal Limited, Park House,
1 Russell Gardens, London NW11 9NN
and
Presidio Press,
P.O. Box 1764, Novato, Ca.94948, U.S.A.

British Library Cataloguing in Publication Data
Mitford, A. B.
Through the Zulu Country: Its
Battlefields and People. – New ed
I. Title
968.4

ISBN 1–85367–116–9

Library of Congress Cataloging-in-Publication Data available
Publishing History
Through the Zulu Country: its Battlefields and its People was
first published in 1883 (Kegan Paul, Trench & Co.). This edition
has been enhanced by the addition of a new Introduction by
Ian Knight, and 19 photographs.

The Publishers wish to acknowledge
with thanks the kind assistance of
Mr. Tony Cracknell, in making available
a copy of the first edition of this book.

Printed and bound in Great Britain by
Biddles Ltd, Guildford and King's Lynn

CONTENTS

—◆◇◆—

CONTENTS

ILLUSTRATIONS

Appearing between pages 134 and 135

——◆◆——

INTRODUCTION.

—◆◇◆—

BERTRAM MITFORD's *Through the Zulu Country: Its Battlefields And Its People*, first published in 1883, is both a classic travelogue, and an invaluable source of eye-witness material on the 1879 Anglo-Zulu War.

The Zulu War has always attracted more than its fair share of public interest, but it comes as something of a surprise to find that tourists were visiting the battlefields within a few years of the last shots being fired. Bertram Mitford was by no means unique; in the 1880s a trickle of adventurers, ex-servicemen and even an eccentric English milady made their way through Zululand's rolling green hills, intent on seeing for themselves the people and places who had, for a time, shaken the British Empire. Perhaps it was eccentric to undertake such a journey at all – Zululand was still a wild and dangerous place, with few roads, and the goodwill of the Zulu people, still suffering the ruinous effects of the war, could hardly have been taken for granted. No doubt each adventure produced its share of traveller's tales, but none of them is in the same league as *Through The Zulu Country*. Mitford was not only possessed of a curious mind and a sharp eye, but he had sufficient talent as a writer to describe his experiences with a freshness which still delights the reader more than a century later.

Bertram Mitford was born on 13th June 1855, the third son of E. L. Osbaldeston Mitford of Mitford Castle, Northumberland. The Mitfords, who trace their descent from Sir John Mitford, a prominent knight in the early fifteenth century, have produced a distinctly literary strain: one branch of the family, ennobled with the title Lord Redesdale, includes the famous Mitford sisters, Jessica, Nancy, Diana, Unity and Deborah. Bertram Mitford's early life appears to have been typical of a young man of his time and class: he was educated at the Royal Naval School, New Cross, and Hurstpierpoint College, Sussex, where he developed a taste for healthy outdoor pursuits, including hiking, shooting and fishing. He travelled to India, East Africa and South Africa in search of adventure as a big-game hunter, and his reputation as a traveller led to him being elected a Fellow of the Royal Geographical Society.

In 1874, like many a younger son of the landed gentry, Mitford looked to the Colonies to make his own way. He went to South Africa to try his hand at stock-farming, but in 1878 gave it up to join the Cape Civil Service. This took him to a number of rural posts, like Fort Beaufort, on the old Cape Frontier. Later, after his first literary successes, he became the proprietor of the *East London Advertiser* between 1886 and 1888. Life in the frontier districts must have been interesting then, since the area had recently been unsettled by a last, mournful uprising by the indigenous Xhosa people: the 1870s and '80s were tough decades for South Africa's black population, as the great kingdoms collapsed one after another in the face of white settler expansion. Mitford was not a military man, and seems to have taken no part in any of these campaigns, but his imagination was clearly fired by the Zulu War. In 1882 he published his first books on the subject; a collection of poems in the patriotic style of the period entitled *Our Arms in Zululand*, and a popular novel, *The Gun-Runner: A Tale of the Zulu War*. *Through the Zulu Country* followed a year later.

Mitford proved a prolific and successful novelist, publishing no less than forty novels and a number of short stories. Most are high adventure yarns; now largely forgotten, they deserve to be considered alongside the better-known works of his contemporaries, Rider Haggard and G. A. Henty. He drew heavily on his own knowledge of southern Africa, and, though he did write about other parts of the world (*Golden Face; A Tale of the Wild West*, 1892, or *The Ruby Sword: A Romance of Baluchistan*, 1898), most of his stories are set against the background of the Cape Frontier, Zulu, Ndebele and Boer Wars. Today, their titles seem hopelessly quaint: *The Weird of Deadly Hollow: A Tale of the Cape Colony* (1891), *'Tween Snow And Fire: A Tale of the Last Kaffir War* (1892), *Renshaw Fanning's Quest: A Tale of the High Veldt* (1894), *Aletta, A Tale of the Boer Invasion* (1900), and *John Ames, Native Commissioner* (1900) are typical. Mitford lacked Haggard's brooding mysticism and his flair for the fantastic, but he was writing for a more adult audience than Henty, and his faults are largely those of the age: his characters are stereotypical, his style is often too flowery for modern tastes, and he occasionally lets slip a gentleman's distaste for the pretensions of frontier society. Nonetheless, he had a firmer grip on historical reality than either Haggard or Henty, his understanding of African peoples was arguably greater, and his novels are still worthwhile reading, not least as insights into contemporary attitudes and opinions.

Bertram Mitford died in 1914, and *Through The Zulu Country* is likely to remain the work by which he is best remembered. Those who come to it as a historical document, or as a traveller's tale, should be equally enchanted. Mitford seems to have been interested in precisely those subjects which would intrigue modern students of the Zulu War in the same circumstances: what evidence of the conflict still lay upon the field in 1882, and what did the Zulus have to say about it?

Through the Zulu Country includes several excellent, apparently verbatim, accounts by ordinary warriors who fought in the great battles: those dealing with Isandlwana are particularly important, and have contributed greatly to our understanding of the battle from the Zulu perspective. In addition, Mitford interviewed many of the leading personalities in Zululand, and he gives us not only an idea of their attitudes and opinions, but a delightful impression of their personalities, which bring them to life like few other sources. He met Sihayo kaXongo, once a powerful border chieftain, now deposed by the British, and his son Mehlokazulu, a subcommander in the iNgobamakhosi regiment, who had fought at the main battles, and 'liked a fight now and then: there was no mistake about it'. He met Prince Dabulamanzi kaMpande, who commanded at Rorke's Drift, Vumandaba kaNtati, one of King Cetshwayo's personal attendants and a commander of the Khandempemvu regiment, and John Dunn, the so-called 'White Chief of the Zulus', who had turned against his former patron Cetshwayo, sided with the British, and been rewarded by them with a slice of the kingdom. Finally, at the end of his journey, Mitford met King Cetshwayo himself, in captivity in Cape Town, and yearning to be allowed to return home.

Not all of these interviews are entirely satisfactory from the reader's point of view: it would be fascinating to hear what Dabulamanzi had to say about Rorke's Drift, but Mitford tells us they 'talked a good deal about the war and subsequent events', but gives us no further details! There is some unconscious humour, too, for having dismissed the Prince as 'an arrant "beggar"', Mitford then tried to persuade him to part with a knobkerry as a souvenir, quite unaware of the irony! Yet, on the whole, Mitford was remarkably free from the worst racial prejudices of his time. He clearly liked and respected the Zulus, which is, perhaps, why their voices still speak with the clear ring of authenticity from his pages.

What's more, Mitford's journey itself took place at a crucial time in Zulu history. The post-war settlement imposed by Sir Garnet Wolseley was on the verge of collapse, and the country was rallying behind pro- and anti-royalist factions. Mitford was aware that trouble was brewing: he heard the rumours of raids and killings, saw a group of armed Zulus hurrying to a muster, and listened to Dunn's earnest plea that the king not be restored. Within a year, of course, Cetshwayo was back in Zululand, and a full-scale civil war would erupt as a consequence.

In the last hundred years, Zululand has changed

considerably from Mitford's day, but the modern
traveller will be struck by the paradox of how much
has nonetheless remained the same. Mitford made
the long haul from England to Durban by sea,
around the Cape: this new edition of *Through The
Zulu Country* excludes his original first chapters,
which are largely taken up with preparations for his
journey and an account of ship-board life, and the
five illustrations, sketches of the sites, which would
have been difficult to re-reproduce today. For this
new edition the book is now illustrated with a
selection of new photographs of the battlefields as
they appear today, chosen to provide an appro-
priate comparison with Mitford's descriptions, and
photographs of Zulus contemporary to Mitford's
visit. The spellings in Mitford's text for various
Zulu names are those that were used until relatively
recent times. However, in the 1940s, Zulu was
scientifically codified as a language and adjustments
have been made to a number of spellings, Isandlwana
(new spelling) being a notable case. Hence for this
Introduction, and in other modern writings, read-
ers may well find different spellings to those which
appeared in contemporary texts.

Flying into the bustling and cosmopolitan city of

Durban today, it is difficult to imagine the still, quiet lagoon, fringed with sub-tropical forest, which greeted the first British traders who arrived to make contact with the Zulus in 1824. From the air, many of the changes which have radically altered the appearance of the landscape are very apparent. Mitford had noted the seeds of them, the introduction of sugar cane and the imported labour from India, which demonstrated the expansion of the Colonial economy. The sugar has long since advanced north across the Thukela into Zululand, and today it covers the corrugated coastal belt like a waving green blanket. Inland, where the climate is less humid, cattle-ranching remains the main agricultural activity, but commercial forestry, mostly imported wattle, checkers the hillsides in geometric blocks. In those areas formerly set aside for the black population, over-crowding and over-grazing have damaged the grass cover, allowing coarse bush to spread, and exposing the top-soil for erosion. Great dongas, or run-off gulleys, scar the hillsides. There are few vistas left of the uninterrupted grassy downlands which Mitford evokes so well, and even by the 1880s much of the wildlife he describes had already been decimated by decades of ruthless exploitation by both black and white hunters. Now, it scarcely exists outside protected game parks.

But, if Zululand's wild spirit has retreated before the advance of progress, at least it is much easier to get around the country. Many of today's tarred highways still follow the old roads of a century ago, their routes dictated by the same geographical limitations. A new extension to the north coast road will slice through the very knoll where the trenches of Fort Pearson are still to be seen, and bridge the Thukela at the same spot where Pearson's column ferried across into Zululand on the day war broke out in January 1879. Further north, the same road bisects the battlefields of Gingindlovu and Nyezane, both of which are submerged beneath the cane; there is still a memorial to Colonel Northey at Gingindlovu, and the spot is just as dismal now as it was in 1882. At Eshowe, where Pearson's men endured four months of siege, there is now a fair sized town, which caters largely for the agricultural community. The trenches and ramparts of Pearson's fort are still there, overgrown with brambles as Mitford saw them, and nearby is the sad little cemetery where his dead were buried. There's

another fort in Eshowe, too: Fort Nongqai, the
barracks of the Zululand Native Police, built in the
1880s in a curiously inappropriate north African
style. Today it houses a small but interesting
museum.

Mitford made his journey to Zululand inland from
Durban, via the provincial capital, Pietermaritz-
burg. 'Maritzburg's imposing buildings still wear a
façade of Colonial elegance, and there's an impressive Zulu War memorial in the town centre. At Fort
Napier, home for decades of the main British garrison in the colony, and now a mental hospital,
Colonel Durnford, of Isandlwana fame, lies in the
cemetery, alongside many a long-forgotten servant
of Empire. The Natal Museum has some interesting
exhibits on Natal life, including a small number of
Zulu War relics. From 'Maritzburg, Mitford trek-
ked up to Greytown, and thence to Helpmekaar,
near the old Zulu border, but his modern counterpart might find it easier to strike north to the
up-country towns of Dundee and Vryheid, both of
which make a useful base for visiting the sites.
Dundee has a good museum, built on the site of the
Boer War battle of Talana, and run by an enthusi-
astic curatrix, Pam McFadden. Vryheid, near the

Transvaal border, has a predominantly Afrikaner atmosphere: it postdates Mitford's visit, having been built on land claimed by the Boers as a reward for their intervention in the Zulu civil wars of the 1880s. Now it lies between the battlefields of Hlobane and Khambula.

Today, Hlobane, which Mitford found so affecting, is owned by a coal mine, and an industrial complex sprawls along part of its base, yet few ever venture up onto the flat windy summit, where Buller's men ran the gauntlet of abaQulusi attacks. The grave of Wood's aides, Captain Campbell and Mr Lloyd, killed by Zulu snipers in the battle, remains untouched, and the energetic hiker can follow a track nearby up onto the summit. The only safe way to visit the infamous Devil's Pass is to walk from here and back, a return journey of about six miles along the top of the mountain. It's worth it; the gently undulating surface is a lost world of low weathered boulders and moorland plants, and the pass itself, a steep jumble of boulders dropping two hundred feet, is an awesome monument to the terrible desperation of the fighting. It's a quiet and haunting place, but sadly, the splendid quiet vistas which so entranced Mitford are more and more disturbed by the spread of workings at the foot of the mountain. He would still recognise Khambula, however, which has hardly been touched by nearby farming activity. 'The tumbledown wall and crumbling earthwork of the fort still crests the mound', though rather lower now than in Mitford's day, and the old cemetery is well cared for. Khambula is a deceptive battlefield; the folds in the ground which played such a key role in the Zulu assault are not immediately apparent from the British position on the ridge, and it repays a few hours spent walking further out. The exposed hillsides still seem to attract the drizzle; on a miserable day it is no less desolate now than Mitford found it.

Mitford struck out to the Zulu border via Greytown and Helpmekaar. Today, it is easier to approach it from the north, for there is little at Helpmekaar to attract any but the most dedicated enthusiast – a collection of derelict buildings, a run-down store and a police station. At Rorke's Drift, Mitford noted that all trace of the fight had been eradicated within three years, and the site of one of the most celebrated battles in British military history is still home for a large mission complex. Recently, however, one of the oldest buildings, which stands on the foundations of the requisitioned hospital, burnt down during the battle, has been opened as a museum. Nearby is the British cemetery, much as Mitford described it, and three monuments mark the site of the mass graves of the Zulu dead.

A few miles downstream from Rorke's Drift is Fugitives' Drift, where a small travellers' lodge nestles in the bush in an ideal setting on the hillsides above the grave of Melvill and Coghill. Run by Zulu War enthusiast David Rattray and his wife Nicky, it is an essential port of call for any visitor, and makes an ideal base from which to visit the sites associated with the Isandlwana campaign. Accommodation is scarce around Zululand, and this one offers a rare opportunity to soak up a little period atmosphere.

Isandlwana, of course, remains the highlight of any battlefield tour. Mitford was struck by its mournful, brooding atmosphere, and the passing of a century, and a steady trickle of visitors, has done nothing to dispel it. There is a new visitors' centre, tastefully incorporated into the old St Vincent's Mission complex, which houses a small museum, and the field itself is dotted with whitewashed cairns which mark the graves of the British dead. On the nek there is a cluster of monuments to the regiments who fell there; George Shepstone's grave is still to be found beneath the western face of the mountain, almost lost amidst the undergrowth and aloes. Until recently, the battlefield debris which Mitford so poignantly describes still came to the surface after a fierce rain, but in the last two decades souvenir hunters have almost stripped the site bare. Recently, they have even damaged memorials and opened graves, and the South African authorities now rigorously prohibit the removal of any relic from any battlefield.

The Zulu people have, of course, changed much since Mitford's time. Though they still cling to many aspects of traditional culture, a century of exposure to the industrialised South African economy has inevitably introduced many western elements. Traditional costume is now very rare, and the old domed thatch huts described by Mitford have given way to square structures of wattle and daub or brick. Ulundi, once the heartland of the old kingdom, where the bones of the unburied dead still lay on the field when Mitford visited, is now the capital of KwaZulu. There's a small but comfortable

Holiday Inn not far from the grave of King Mpande, and across the rolling plain, where the Zulu regiments once charged to their destruction, now heavily settled and bisected by a railway line, King Cetshwayo's old homestead has arisen from the ashes. Archaeologists have restored part of it, now known by its alternative name, Ondini, and nearby stands the KwaZulu Cultural Museum. The spot where Lord Chelmsford's square stood during the final battle of the war is marked by a stone archway topped by a silver dome, where plaques commemorate the heroism of both sides.

Many tourists today visit the principal battlefields of Zululand, but it is worth taking time, as Mitford did, to linger and explore off the beaten track. The traces of half-forgotten British camps, low parapets and shallow trenches in the grass, can still be found beside the old lines of advance, and there are other, sadder, milestones left in history's wake, the pathetic clusters of graves and cairns of those who fell in dimly-remembered skirmishes, or died of disease whilst on campaign. Lieutenant Pardoe, who succumbed to wounds received at Ulundi, still lies in his lonely grave near Fort Marshall, and Zulu cattle graze outside the enclosure where Lieutenant Frith, killed in a skirmish, was buried at Fort Newdigate. Lieutenant Scott Douglas and his escort, Corporal Cotter, whose story is told by Mitford, lie side-by-side beneath shadey trees by a farmhouse at KwaMagwaza. The Queen's Cross still marks the spot where the Prince Imperial was killed, dwarfing the graves of Troopers Abel and Rogers, though the Prince himself is not even buried there. Remember, too, that the events of 1879 are only one year in the rich heritage of Zulu history, and the dramatic and beautiful countryside is littered with reminders of the nation's extraordinary story. King Shaka, who founded the Zulu kingdom, lies buried at Stanger, near the coast, and the royal homestead of his successor Dingane has been partially restored at Mgungundlovu, south of the White Mfolozi. At Blood River, where the Boers defeated the Zulus in December 1838, there is a striking monument, a circle of life-sized wagons cast in bronze. Once it was only the British and Afrikaners who put up monuments in Zululand: now the Zulus themselves are remembering their own monarchs and heroes.

Bertram Mitford was amongst the first to feel the allure which has drawn travellers to Zululand ever since. For many, it can be a moving experience, something of a pilgrimage. As the Zulus say, '*Hamba Gahle* – Go Well.'

*

Anyone wishing to visit the Zulu War sites is advised to go armed with a copy of John Laband and Paul Thompson's *Field Guide To The War In Zululand And The Defence Of Natal, 1879*, published by the University of Natal. This consists of a detailed series of maps which are invaluable when it comes to locating sites and identifying features. My thanks to Tony Cracknell, who has been 'through the Zulu country' with me, for making his copy of Mitford's first edition available for this reprint, and to Rai England, also a veteran traveller, for the photograph of Mitford which has been used on the dust jacket.

IAN KNIGHT
Canterbury, 1992

CHAPTER I

Off to the Border—Grey Town—'Blue gums'—Bush scenery—The
Tugela—An aquatic dilemma—Sunrise on the Biggarsberg
Heights—A model road—Rorke's Drift, past and present.

At first it seems rather slow work rolling tediously
along on a hot afternoon at the rate of three or
four miles an hour, but I soon fall into it and sit
on the waggon box, pipe in mouth, with all the
stoicism of an old 'trekker.' A short outspan
towards sundown, on again, and suddenly—for
there is little or no twilight in Southern Africa—
drops the curtain of night; the stars shine out one
by one, the hills loom black against the liquid sky,
yonder a twinkling light points to the whereabouts
of some homestead standing in its group of blue
gums, while here and there a distant grass fire glows
red upon the far horizon. All is still, save for
the whistle of a flight of plover, which startled from
the ground by the tramp of my horse's feet, circle
overhead sounding their shrill pipes; while now
and then the rumble of the waggon as it crawls
slowly over the hills behind, or the harsh shout of

the driver to his span, comes faintly on the silence
of the night.   Presently the sky brightens, the
outlines of the hills assume more definite shape,
the heavens are suffused with a gathering flush,
and a golden moon rises, gently flooding the open
sweeping landscape far and near.   And now I hear
the murmur and plashing of a river ; the walls of
a few houses shimmer white in the moonlight ; I
have reached the Umgeni bridge, twelve miles
from Maritzburg, so dismounting I await the
arrival of the waggon and outspan for the night.
But it is a short rest.   Long before sunrise we are
on the road again ; and avoiding the midday heat
and travelling by night and in the early morning,
we reach Grey Town the following day.

If asked what struck me as the most prominent
feature of Grey Town I should inevitably reply
' Blue gums,' for the blue gum is everywhere—in
the gardens, along the streets, sheltering the home-
steads, dropped about the hillsides—lines upon
lines of this useful and ornamental tree, giving
quite a snug appearance to the village, which otherwise would stand bare and commonplace upon an
open plain.   The native name for Grey Town is
Mkunkundhlovwane, ' Little Maritzburg,' being the
diminutive of their name for the capital, of which
the place looks like a minimised version.   Put more
idiomatically it might be rendered ' Maritzburg on
a small scale.'

But I must find my third ' hand.' Here again, however, all the old difficulties crop up. Plenty of ' boys ' are ready to engage, but are deficient in the very first qualification ; others, again, who would be just what I wanted, are out of the way for the time being, nor does anyone know how or where to get at them. At last, thanks to the kind and valuable assistance of Mr. Mansel, the officer in command of the Natal Mounted Police at Grey Town, I succeed in securing the services of a likely-looking ' boy ' with a sufficient knowledge of English, and in other respects a quiet, good-tempered, willing fellow. At early dawn we are on the move, toiling slowly up the long hill away from Grey Town, and by the time it begins to wax unpleasantly warm we halt on a beautiful spot at the entrance to ' the thorns.' Andries, the Grey Town ' boy,' has fraternised with the driver and leader—natives ' chum ' very readily—and has had an opportunity of making himself useful, so that when we inspan late in the afternoon, as the sun's rays begin to abate their fierceness, everything is square and promising for the trip.

And now the country, which hitherto has been open and wholly destitute of bush, suddenly assumes a very different aspect. Thick vegetation covers the valley into which we are descending, and far as the eye can reach the wooded slopes

stretch away, purple and dim in the afternoon
haze.   The road winds round the spurs in its
gradual descent, becoming wilder and more rugged.
On the one hand a mighty precipice rears its red
wall, pierced with holes and caves like so many
black spots upon its surface; there a mass of
gigantic crags piled against the sky-line like the
turrets of a stately castle; further on, a huge rock
stands out in solitary ruggedness amid the surroundings of the dark green bush.   Birds of brilliant
plumage are winging in and out among the aloes
and mimosa trees; the clear whistle of the spreuw [1]
peals with many an echo from yon frowning cliff;
while far away down the valley is heard the soft
'cooing' of hundreds of turtledoves.   Nor is
insect life wanting; the cicala's constant chirp and
the whirr of a large winged locust, the gnat's
shrill horn and the loud booming hum of a big
beetle—all blend harmoniously in the swell of
Nature's evening chorus.   Now we dip down
almost out of sight to cross the deep bed of a trickling watercourse—up again, but everywhere mountain and valley, towering cliff, bush-clad slope and
black ravine; a panorama of Nature in her wildest
and most fantastic aspect.   But hark! the distant
barking of a dog and the low of cattle.   Not even
these familiar sounds tell of approaching civilisa-

[1] A bird of the starling tribe.

tion, for picturesquely situated on yonder spur is a
native kraal, its beehive-shaped huts standing in
a circle round the cattle enclosure—meet abode of
savage man, in keeping with his wild surroundings.

Nearer and nearer dips the sun to the overhanging mountain tops, the outlines of the hills
start forth sharp and defined from the haze which
has hitherto toned them down, and the effects of
light and shade are perfect. Yonder a distant cliff
gleams like a wall of burnished bronze rising from
an emerald-covered slope, as the slanting beams
strike full upon its smooth surface; another, which
hitherto has been all in the light, now falls back
into gloom, throwing its long black shadow beneath,
as though sullenly resenting the fickle desertion of
the glorious sun. And the night falls. Star after
star, with many a flashing constellation, quivers in
the vault above, and the Southern Cross shines
upon the lonely traveller like a candelabrum of
golden lamps. A nightjar rises and skims overhead uttering its whirring note; the bark of a
prowling jackal far away in the thorns is borne
upon the stillness; every now and then a big
beetle, whizzing with loud hum through the warm
air, blunders into my face as I ride along; fireflies
glint among the bushes in many a floating spark,
but not a sound or sight which tells of the presence
of man—the night side of Nature in her own soli-

tudes.   Dismounting, I sit by the roadside in
the gloom and await the waggon.   A large
hare sidles out of the bush and ambles con-
tentedly along the road ; true to the British
instinct of destructiveness I pick up a stone and
launch it at the unsuspecting quadruped, but my
improvised missile does not take effect,—and there
is the waggon coming round the bend, so resigning
my pony to Andries I climb on to the box.   We
plod slowly but merrily along, for my retainers are
cheerful fellows, and sing, chat, and laugh with five-
hundred-lung power.   A couple of hours more
and we are at the Mooi River Drift, forming one of
a group of waggons there outspanned, whose fires
throw a red flickering glare on the surrounding
bush.   It is late; so after tying the oxen to the
yokes, getting the kettle into play and disposing of
the contents of the same, my sable retinue rolls itself in its blanket and turns in, an example which
after our long ' trek ' I am not ill-disposed to follow,
and know no more till awoke to consciousness at
dawn by sundry forcible and time-honoured ejacu-
lations attendant upon inspanning, as my neighbours
of the previous night are making a start.   We do
likewise, but before we reach the high ridge
between Mooi River and the Tugela the sun has
been up some time and the result is not stimulating.
Once over the ridge the rest of the way is down

hill. A long straight bit of road, where we seem poised, as on a ledge, over the valley beneath, affords a magnificent view ; then the descent begins, and bump, bump—a long slide—a lurch first to this side then to that—more bumping, and after two hours or so of toilsome descent into a hot valley we halt at the Tugela Drift to recruit, if haply one may find rest and shade in such a sweltering hole.

Now there is on the Tugela at that point an efficient pontoon, which, the drift being a remarkably bad one, is usually in requisition. I, having had a good deal of experience in crossing South African rivers, ought to have known better ; but thinking that the drift, though broad, was probably smooth and shallow, went at it most confidingly, voting the pontoon unnecessary in the present instance. The result was melancholy. In rolled the waggon pleasantly enough till nearly in mid-stream—at that point more than 150 yards wide—and there suddenly stuck. The water became deeper and deeper ; the current running so strong that the leader could barely keep his feet, and the whole turn-out was in imminent jeopardy of going down stream. In vain we shouted and yelled ; in vain we plied whip and thong upon the obdurate hides of the recalcitrant team ; in vain we exhausted all the forcible and suggestive phraseology in the vocabulary of the road, and began again; there we stuck. What was to be done? Turning back was a physical impossibility, and the oxen began to plunge and get more and more unmanageable, for, bending back their heads in order to keep their noses above the surface, the poor brutes were half strangled by the yoke-straps. The water was already flowing over the footboard; an inch deeper and the waggon would be flooded, which meant that my supplies for the trip would be seriously damaged, if not absolutely spoilt. In despair I tried another plan. Could we but keep the oxen quiet for a few moments, the short rest might get us through provided the water became no deeper. Again the whips crack like pistol shots—a sudden pull, the oxen feel their feet—another sudden and more violent tug, and we roll out; a couple of minutes more and we are on the other side breathless and exhausted, the steam ascending in clouds from the dripping flanks of the panting span. But I there and then register a vow that nothing on earth will induce me again to tempt that execrable drift, unless the water is very low indeed.

About eighteen miles beyond the Tugela is the seat of magistracy for the border division of Umsinga. Calling on the resident magistrate,

Mr. Fynn, I was most kindly received, and not having yet been long enough on my travels to get used to my own company, but quite long enough to be rather tired of the same, I was able thoroughly to enjoy spending an evening in civilised fashion with that hospitable official. Pushing on again the following afternoon, we halted at nightfall near the top of the Biggarsberg ridge, expecting to make Rorke's Drift the next day.

The moon is still shining brightly as we inspan for an early start, and not until we are well on the road do the stars begin to pale, but the morning is cold and raw. As we 'trek' along the ridge a sight peculiar to mountainous country bursts upon the view. The road is clear, but a hundred yards or so to the right the ground falls abruptly into a vast and unbroken mass of fleecy cloud, white as driven snow. Presently a heavy film of mist steals up from below, growing thicker and thicker, till we are moving along through the raw fog, and seem to enter again into darkness, but not for long; as the sun rises the mist rolls back, hanging in silver curtains over the sparkling ground, and many a tiny rainbow flashes its prismatic hues as the sunbeams cleave the dewy vapour. And now the sun is well up; the dense masses of billowy cloud stretch away from one's very feet; the road winds over a narrow neck as through a gate, opening upon a fresh expanse of country, which at present, however, is completely veiled. The firmament is a beautifully clear greenish-blue above the dazzling whiteness; birds are singing on all sides, and every blade of grass gleams and sparkles with myriads of liquid diamonds.

The whole valley of the Buffalo and the country beyond the Zulu border is veiled in thick impenetrable cloud, and Helpmakaar, for all practical purposes, seems still under the influence of the drowsy god. But I am in want of information as to the road, so proceed summarily to knock up one of the inhabitants, and learn that there are two roads to Rorke's Drift, both infamously bad; in fact little to choose between them, save in point of distance, the shortest being twelve miles, the other about twice as long. No huge amount of inductive ratiocination being required to perceive that twenty-four miles of iniquitously bad road is worse than twelve of ditto, I elect to take the shortest and chance it.

Helpmakaar,[1] which it will be remembered was an important depôt during the Zulu war, is on the main road to Newcastle, and is situated on one of the highest ridges of the Biggarsberg,

[1] A Dutch word meaning ' help each other.'

commanding a wide sweep of open country on
either side. It consists of three or four houses
and a few shanties, including an 'hotel,' and
boasts a post office agency. The entrenchment
still remains—a solid-looking earthwork surrounded
by a fosse ; close by is a little cemetery containing
the graves of those officers and men who succumbed to exposure and fatigue while at that
bleak station. Here, too, fled the fugitives from
Isandhlwana, and at last I felt that I was actually
on historic ground.

I said that the road thence to Rorke's Drift
was infamously bad, and in saying so I have fallen
far short of adequately describing it. All was
well enough till the steep part of the descent
began, and then—huge stones, boulders, pebbles,
rocks large and rocks small, heaped one upon
another or lying strewn about ; the actual road-
way as uneven as a dry watercourse — bump,
bump, bump, the order of the day. Again and
again I thought the waggon must inevitably break
to pieces as the wheels on one side were poised
high in air, grinding over a huge stone, those on
the other crashing violently into a deep rut, and
the whole fabric literally twisting and writhing as
though it had life. But marvellous is the elasticity
of these vehicles ; I was nearly saying that india-
rubber was a joke thereto, for twenty times as

I rode along did I expect to see the whole structure fairly wrenched asunder; however, we reached the plain below with little more damage than the starting of a bolt or two, and again I breathed freely.

From the brow of the hill just before descending, Isandhlwana comes into view, standing out in rugged boldness from the surrounding heights, towering grim and dark in the summer haze like a huge lion,[1] but the glimpse is little more than a momentary one, and is lost to sight as the road makes a sudden dip. In front the Buffalo threads along, past Rorke's Drift and the Bashi valley, and the open plain stretches away beyond the Blood River, far into the Transvaal territory. A silent and desert expanse; on the right a semi-gloom, where the frowning cliffs overhanging the Bashi valley cast their shadows; not a sign of life anywhere—a lonely and unprotected border.

It was late in the afternoon as we descended to the plain. A couple of tall blue gums rising above a slight eminence mark the site of the famous post; in front again appears the stern shape of Isandhlwana, its precipitous wall clear and distinct in the setting sun. Riding on I soon reached the post. The post, did I say? Few or no traces of the old fortifications were to be seen,

---

[1] From whatever point you look at it, Isandhlwana wears the shape of a lion *couchant*.

but a large house was in course of construction, the residence of Mr. Otto Witt, the Swedish missionary, whose name, it may be remembered, was before the public at the beginning of the war. Much carpentering and joining was going on in the verandah; outhouses stood around, hard by was the chapel belonging to the Mission, but of the defences not a trace. Save for the little cemetery, where are lying the few who fell of that handful of gallant defenders, it would be difficult to realise that one stood on the site of the most brilliant feat of arms of our day. To the cemetery I passed; a modest burial ground enclosed by a sod wall, the names of its silent denizens graven on an obelisk in the midst.

The sun had sunk behind the western ridges, the shadows of evening were creeping over a cloudless sky, and as I stood among the grass-grown graves the events of that memorable night seemed to rise up one by one. There was the conical hill overhanging the post, round whose base the enemy first appeared; the ledge of rocks a couple of hundred yards off, from which his sharp-shooters harassed our position till dislodged by the heavy fire of our men. I said that all traces of the fortifications had disappeared, yet would imagination supply deficiencies; the outer and inner lines of defence, the site of the hospital— and I seemed to see the terrific rush of the savage

hosts as they swarmed up to the breastwork, the
desperately determined faces of its defenders, the
smoke and crash of volleys, the lurid flames of
the burning hospital and the ghastly countenances
of its inmates as they are brought out one by one,
the gleam of a forest of blades in the red light.
Still could I hear the clash of assegai and shield
splintered by bayonet thrusts dealt with all the
fury of men fighting for their lives, the 'thud'
of falling bodies, the ringing shots, the reckless
British hurrah mingled with the fierce 'Usútu'[1]
pealing from 4,000 savage throats as again and
again the columns of maddened Zulu warriors
poured on to the attack—to use their own
metaphor—'seeing nothing but blood!'

But my reverie is broken in upon by the sound
of wheels, and looking up I discover that the
waggon is close at hand, so betake myself forthwith to the drift, which is nearly a quarter of a
mile distant from the post. I would fain cross
to-night, but am unacquainted with the idiosyn-
crasies of the said drift; the oxen have had a long
day of it, and I have no fancy for a repetition
of the Tugela entertainment : moreover it is nearly
dark, so I conclude to outspan and defer crossing
till the morrow.

[1] The Zulu war cry.

CHAPTER II

MORNING. The summer sun has dispersed the
chill folds of a heavy mist, and his cheering rays
fall upon as pleasant a scene as one could wish
to cast eye over. Across a charming bit of country does my first stage in Zululand lead, steep and
stony in parts, in others smooth and undulating,
but everywhere green and smiling, for these are
well-watered regions, and you cannot go far
without coming upon a spring or a stream of some
sort. On the right the Buffalo makes a bend
round the base of Shiyane, the conical bushy
mountain overlooking Rorke's Drift, and a high
rugged range rises on the Natal side of the river—
in front Isandhlwana—on the left a long array of
precipitous rocks overhanging the beautiful valley
of the Bashi, and presently we cross the river of
that name; a shallow limpid stream bubbling
along over its sandy bottom. But signs of habita-

tion now begin to show ; a mealie patch here and there, cattle grazing among the thorns, then larger mealie gardens in which women are at work, and on the hillside stands a well-to-do-looking kraal. A fine athletic native trots past, hurling his cheery greeting 'Inkos!' (Chief) over his shoulder as he runs. A picturesque object is he, tall and lithe as a bronze Apollo ; a few fantastic ornaments of beadwork and hide constitute his attire, a long reed snuff-box is stuck through the lobe of his ear, and in his hand the inevitable knob-kerrie.

At last we dip down into the valley through which swept the right horn of the Zulu army to cut off retreat by the Rorke's Drift road. A clear stream is brawling along over rocks and stones, birds are whistling among the aloes and mimosa bushes, and in front the western cliff of Isandhl-wana heaves high in air. I ride up the slope and gain the 'neck'; on the right is the small stony hillock known as 'Black's Kopje,' and Fugitives' Track, a scarcely discernible path, leading away from it into the thorns ; the huge crag, now towering immediately overhead, casts a long dark shadow on the plain, whose stillness is only broken by the hum of a passing insect or the chirp of a small bird in the grass, and amid the hush of the summer afternoon all the associations of the spot seem to crowd up thick and fast. There on the right is a high cairn of stones, marking the spot where Colonel Durnford, Lieutenant Scott, and the Natal Carbineers made their last stand ; near this a few graves, the remains of whose occupants are partly uncovered through the wasting away of the soil by rains ; lower down, an obelisk, a tombstone or two, and mounds of earth mark the resting places of more victims of that disastrous day, and a little below the ' neck ' stands the iron cross erected by the Bishop of Maritzburg on the occasion of his holding a funeral service there.

I ride over the camp ground, and although three years have elapsed, there is no lack of traces of the melancholy struggle. In spite of a luxuriant growth of herbage the circles where stood the rows of tents are plainly discernible, while strewn about are tent pegs, cartridge cases, broken glass, bits of rope, meat tins and sardine boxes pierced with assegai stabs, shrivelled up pieces of shoe-leather, and rubbish of every description ; bones of horses and oxen gleam white and ghastly, and here and there in the grass one stumbles upon a half-buried skeleton. From the back of the camp ground rises a steep slope, covered with stones and boulders, and culminating in the rocky wall which rears itself to a height of four hundred feet above the plain. A striking and remarkable mount is

Isandhlwana, not another hill around is there in the least like it; in fact the only one resembling it in any degree is the Zihlalu, between Ulundi and Inhlazatye, which, however, is on a much larger scale. I have already alluded to the lion-like shape of Isandhlwana, and it is not a little curious that it should also resemble the sphinx badge of the 24th Regiment. I showed one of these badges, picked up on the field, to a Zulu warrior who had taken part in the battle, and drew his attention to the coincidence. He gave a start and ejaculation of astonishment, and shook his head in deprecation of the ' uncanniness ' of the whole proceeding.

St. Vincent's Mission, the residence and head-quarters of the Bishop of Zululand, stands on the north side of the camp ground, at the foot of the steep range over which the main body of the enemy came—a substantial stone house, a few huts, some strips of cultivated land, and a stone enclosure or two for cattle and horses. There is no regular ' location,' the only natives living on the station being those employed in house or farm work in connection therewith—a move in the right direction, for anyone who has travelled in South Africa will bear me out in saying that among the tumble-down ill-built huts of mission and town locations, dirt and squalor reign to an extent unknown in the ordinary native kraals, which are, as a rule, singularly neat and tidy. The community at St. Vincent's consisted of the Bishop and his household, two clergymen and a lay schoolmaster, a farm overseer, and a few colonial boys training for mission work—about a dozen Europeans in all. Not by any means a luxurious or easy life is that of these missionaries. Frequent services, kraal visiting, school duties, and manual labour in the field, all this keeps their time thoroughly occupied from early morning till dark and after. Nor is accommodation sumptuous; one of them had nothing more commodious for a sleeping apartment and study than a small native hut, another had made a bedroom of the Bishop's travelling waggon. The mission house too is plainly furnished, but his lordship is very mindful of the apostolic injunction, and hospitality forms a real item in the St. Vincent's programme. The Sunday services were many, and mostly in the Zulu language; there was no church, but a room had been fitted up to do duty for it, and at one end, on a raised footpace, stood an altar, duly garnished with a large cross and a pair of candlesticks. It struck me that Bishop McKenzie in his alb and chasuble looked far more episcopal than his English *confrères* in the meaningless, balloon-sleeved vesture so dear to the heart of the Anglican prelate, and that the service was more calculated to impress the heathen with a sense of dignity and importance. There being no harmonium, the singing was unaccompanied, and when in the course of it a stray ' click ' occurred, the effect was not a little curious to uninitiated ears. But I thought I had never heard a language which suited the Divine Office better than this sonorous and musical tongue. There was a service specially for heathen, on which occasion the room was well filled, mostly with men from kraals in the neighbourhood, who listened attentively and respectfully to the ' Umfundisi ; ' [1] whether they really took in what was told them is quite another thing, for it is no easy matter to convince the shrewd, sceptical Zulu. He will listen patiently and courteously enough—for he has all the instincts of a gentleman—while in his heart of hearts he is thinking ' there is not much in it ; ' or he will shake his head with a deprecatory smile, which might be interpreted ' *Umfundisi* is a good man, but——.' While on the subject of missions and missionaries, an idea seems to have got hold of the religious world that the first thing to do with a native is to clothe him—in fact, that until he can be induced to wear breeches his Christianity is worth very little indeed. Let anyone doubting this look at the first missionary periodical at

[1] Teacher or missionary.

hand :—' The natives take readily to clothes '— 'the people are all asking for clothes'—such are the statements that will meet the eye, as if the sudden development of a taste for tailoring among a dark-skinned race in a sweltering climate was a sure sign of grace. The Zulu in his normal garb (which is far more decent than that of most savages), his supple limbs modelled like those of a bronze statue, striding along with head erect and light elastic step, is a fine noble-looking fellow ; clap a tweed suit and shirt collar upon him, not omitting a chimney-pot hat, or even a wideawake, and you turn him into an awkward ungainly barbarian, looking and feeling thoroughly ridiculous and uncomfortable. Wherefore the question arises—Can these people be intended to wear clothes ?

A practical difficulty which meets the missionary at every turn is polygamy, a custom so deeply rooted in the national institutions as to be an almost insurmountable barrier to the spread of Christianity. The Zulu gains in position and importance according to the number of his wives, for these represent value received for so many head of cattle paid away, which in turn constitute riches ; and over and above the actual loss of their labour in the tillage of the soil, a man of position would hardly undergo the ridicule and social degrada-

tion which the putting away of his women would
involve. Nor is it by any means sure that these
good ladies would take the matter quietly—and
' curtain influence ' counts for something even in
Zululand—the cant that has been talked about the
oppressed and down-trodden state of the women
notwithstanding, on which subject, by the way, it
struck me, during my progress through the country,
that they wore anything but a crushed appearance.
I heard the above difficulty discussed by the
missionaries, who themselves seemed by no means
clear as to the solution of the question, but with
them I shall now leave it.

Bishop McKenzie is a tall, dark man in the
prime of life, and gifted with a strong voice and
good delivery. As to his energy there can be no
sort of doubt. He is at work from morning till
night at one thing or another, and periodically
makes Visitation tours throughout his somewhat
extensive diocese ; at the time of my leaving
Zululand he was on the point of starting upon
one of these, to extend far away beyond the Swazi
country, a matter of several weeks. An isolated
life is this missionary life, unendurable for any
length of time save to those whose hearts are in
the work. To the hard-worked priest toiling in the
slums of our teeming cities the free air and sun-

shine, the great mountains and silent wastes of a wild country, may seem a pleasant relief to turn to. But I question whether the isolation would not counterbalance other attractions and advantages when put to the test.

CHAPTER III

Meaning of 'Isandhlwana '—Zulu narratives of the battle.

THE site of the camp is along the eastern base of Isandhlwana,[1] which rises immediately above it in the rear; fronting it the country is all open to Isipezi mountain, some fourteen miles off, where Lord Chelmsford was engaging Matyana at the time of the attack. On the left, but at right angles to Isandhlwana, which lies north and south, runs the Nqutu range, over which the Zulu army first appeared. At the foot of this range, about two miles from camp, is a conical eminence where the rocket battery was stationed. The actual scene of operations, then, was an oblong plain about three miles in extent, whence, in the event of defeat, escape would only be possible by making for the

[1] The meaning of Isandhlwana, or more correctly Isandhlwane, is neither ' little hand,' nor ' little house,' nor any other of the hundred and one interpretations which were devised at the time of the disaster, but refers to a portion of bovine intestinal anatomy. The spelling of the word which I shall observe throughout these pages will be that which is now universally employed, though ' Isandhlwane' is the more correct. The pronunciation of the word is exactly according to its orthography, every letter being distinctly sounded.

river some miles off on the right, or by gaining the
Rorke's Drift road over the ' neck ' in the rear.
The slope round the actual base of Isandhlwana
is steep and rugged, and intersected with deep
' dongas ' here and there, the rest of the plain
being fairly smooth.

The following narrative is that of a warrior of
the Umbonambi regiment, who was present at the
battle ; I give it as nearly as possible in his own
words :—

'Several days before the fight we started from
Undini, eight regiments strong (about 25,000 men).
The King said, " The white soldiers have crossed
into Zululand and are coming further in, soon
they will be here (at Undini) ; go and drive them
across Umzinyati (the Buffalo) right back into
Natal." The *impi* [1] was commanded by Tyingwayo ;
under him were Mavumengwane, Mundúla, and
Vumandaba, the *induna* (chief) of the Kandam-
pemvu regiment ; this regiment is also called
Umcityu, but Kandampemvu is the oldest name.
Matyana-ka-Mondisi was not present, nor was
Dabulamanzi. Untuswa, brother of Seketwayo, is
the *induna* of my regiment ; he took part in the
fight, so did Mehlo-ka-zulu and Sirayo's other son.
The chief Sibepu also fought.

[1] A body of men under arms for any military or aggressive
purpose.

'We were lying in the hills up there, when one of our scouting parties came back followed by a number of mounted men ; they were most of them natives, but some were whites. They fired upon us. Then the whole *impi* became very excited and sprang up. When the horsemen saw how numerous we were they began to retreat. We formed up in rank and marched towards the camp. At the top of the last hill we were met by more horsemen, but we were too many for them and they retreated. Here, where we are standing (my informant's kraal was situated close to the rocket hill before mentioned), there were some parties of soldiers in red coats who kept up a heavy fire upon us as we came over. My regiment was here and lost a lot of men ; they kept tumbling over one upon another. (The narrator became quite excited, and indulged in much gesticulation, illustrating the volleys by cracking his fingers like pistol-shots.) Then the Ngobamakosi regiment, which formed the left horn of the *impi*, extended and swept round on the south of the rocket hill so as to outflank the soldiers, who, seeing this, fell back and took cover in that donga[1] (pointing to a donga which inter-

---

[1] These dongas are rifts in the ground caused by heavy rains, and varying in depth from two to fifty feet. So suddenly do they occur that where you thought all was smooth and unbroken, you find yourself on the brink of a yawning chasm, which perhaps will necessitate a détour of several miles.

sects the field about a mile from camp), and fired
upon us from there. By that time the Ngobamakosi had got among the " paraffin " (rockets) and
killed the horses, and were circling round so as to
shut in the camp on the side of the river, but *we*
could not advance, the fire from the donga was
too heavy. The great *indunas* were on the hill
over there (pointing to an eminence commanding
the north side of the camp, above where the mis-
sion-house now stands), and just below them a
number of soldiers were engaging the Kandampemvu regiment, which was being driven back, but
one of the sub-chiefs of the Kandampemvu ran
down from the hill and rallied them, calling out that
they would get the whole *impi* beaten and must
come on. Then they all shouted " Usútu ! " and
waving their shields charged the soldiers with great
fury. The chief was shot through the forehead and
dropped down dead, but the Kandampemvu rushed
over his body and fell upon the soldiers, stabbing
them with their assegais and driving them right in
among the tents.

'My regiment and the Umpunga formed the
centre of the *impi*. When the soldiers in the
donga saw that the Kandampemvu were getting
behind them, they retreated upon the camp, firing
at us all the time. As they retreated we followed
them. I saw several white men on horseback

galloping towards the "neck," which was the only
point open; then the Nokenke and Nodwengu
regiments, which had formed the right horn of the
impi, joined with the Ngobamakosi on the "neck."
After that there was so much smoke that I could
not see whether the white men had got through or
not. The tumult and the firing was wonderful;
every warrior shouted "Usútu!" as he killed anyone, and the sun got very dark,[1] like night, with
the smoke. The English fought long and hard;
there were so many of our people in front of me
that I did not get into the thick of the fight until
the end. The warriors called out that all the white
men had been killed, and then we began to plunder
the camp. The Undi and Udhloko regiments,
which had been in reserve, then went on "kwa
Jim"[2] to take the post there. We found "tywala"[3]
in the camp, and some of our men got very drunk.
We were so hot and thirsty that we drank everything liquid we found, without waiting to see what
it was. Some of them found some black stuff in
bottles (probably ink); it did not look good, so they
did not drink it; but one or two who drank some

---

[1] He is referring to an annular eclipse, which, it is not a little
curious, should have taken place while the frightful conflict was at its
height.

[2] Literally, 'at Jim's.' Rorke's Drift is so called by the Zulus after
one 'Jim' Rorke, who formerly lived there.

[3] Native beer. The word is also applied to ardent spirits or any
sort of intoxicating beverage.

paraffin oil, thinking it was "tywala," were poisoned. We took as much plunder as we could carry, and went away home to our kraals. We did not re-assemble and march back to Ulundi.

'At first we had not intended attacking the camp that day, as the moon was "wrong" (in an unfavourable quarter—a superstition), but as the whites had discovered our presence the *indunas* said we had better go on. Only six regiments took part in the fight—the Nodwengu, Nokenke, Umbonambi, Umpunga, Kandampemvu, and Ngobamakosi. The Uve is part of the Ngo-bamakosi, and not a separate corps; it is the boys' regiment.'

The above seems a plain unvarnished version of those events of the day which came within the narrator's actual observation; the following account is that of a Zulu belonging to the Nokenke regiment, which, with the Nodwengu, formed the right horn of the attacking force, and operated at the back of Isandhlwana moun-tain. The first portion of the narrative, as to how the affair began, tallies exactly with that of the Umbonambi warrior, albeit the men were unknown to each other, for I picked up this story in a different part of the country. After describing the earlier movements, he went on :—

'While the Kandampemvu were driving back the horsemen over the hill north of the camp, we worked round behind Isandhlwana under cover of the long grass and dongas, intending to join with the Ngobamakosi on the "neck" and sweep in upon the camp. Then we saw white men beginning to run away along the road "kwa Jim;" many of these were cut off and killed, down in the stream which flows through the bottom of the valley. More and more came over, some mounted and some on foot. When they saw that the valley was full of our warriors, they turned to the left and ran off along the side of the hill towards Umzinyati (the Buffalo); those who had not got horses were soon overtaken. The Nodwengu pursued the mounted men, numbers of whom were killed among the thorns and dongas, but I heard that some escaped. Our regiment went over into the camp. The ground is high and full of dongas and stones, and the soldiers did not see us till we were right upon them. They fought well—a lot of them got up on the steep slope under the cliff behind the camp, and the Zulus could not get at them at all ; they were shot or bayoneted as fast as they came up. At last the soldiers gave a shout and charged down upon us. There was an *induna* [1] in front of them with a long flashing sword, which he whirled round his head as he ran—it must have been made of fire.

[1] Supposed to be Captain Younghusband.

Wheugh ! (Here the speaker made an expressive gesture of shading the eyes.). They killed themselves by running down, for our people got above them and quite surrounded them ; these, and a group of white men on the " neck," were the last to fall.

'The sun turned black in the middle of the battle ; we could still see it over us, or should have thought we had been fighting till evening. Then we got into the camp, and there was a great deal of smoke and firing. Afterwards the sun came out bright again.'—' Were there any prisoners taken ? ' I asked.—' No ; all were killed on the field, and at once ; no white men were tortured : it is the Zulu custom to kill everyone on the spot ; prisoners are never taken.'

There seems no reason for doubting this statement, which may be taken as scattering to the winds the numerous absurd and sensational 'yarns' which got about at the time, and are still credited. Several Zulus whom I questioned on the subject all agreed in saying that it was not the custom to torture prisoners of war, though it was sometimes done in cases of ' umtagati ' (witchcraft). Hence it is comforting to know that our unfortunate countrymen who fell on that fatal day were spared the most horrible side of savage warfare, and met their deaths as soldiers, in the thick of battle, at the hands of a foe in every respect worthy of their steel.

CHAPTER IV

ONE morning I started from Isandhlwana to explore
the line of retreat to 'Fugitives' Drift,' as it is now
called, accompanied by one of the mission clergy,
who had kindly offered to act as guide. Riding
over the camp ground we crossed the waggon road
on the 'neck,' and struck into the narrow path
running along the base of 'Black's Kopje' down
into the ravine. Heaps of *débris* lay about—bones
and skulls of oxen, belt buckles, sardine tins,
shrivelled-up boots, the nails falling out of the
rotting soles, odds and ends of clothing, old
brushes—in fact, rubbish of all sorts; while every
ten or twenty yards we would come upon sadder
traces of the flight in the shape of little heaps of
stones, through the interstices of which could be
seen the bones of some unfortunate buried under-
neath. The track is smooth enough for three or

four hundred yards, and then the trouble begins ; as we get among the thorns the ground is seamed with deep dongas yawning suddenly before us, rendering riding anything but safe. Now we are on the brink of one of these chasms ; then the track suddenly diverging, takes us along a narrow razor-like ridge with a fall of some fifteen or twenty feet on either side. I pictured to myself what long odds were against a lot of men riding for their lives over such ground, all crowding upon each other, and the savage enemy behind rushing in among them with unearthly yells, driving the maddened horses into the dongas and stabbing their riders—and many seemed to have come to grief here, judging from the traces. At the bottom of one of these fissures lay the fragments of an ammunition train, which had evidently taken a regular ' header,' the shattered skeletons of four horses or mules in a heap together, and thinly covered over with stones those of the two unfortunates who presumably were with the team. Among twisted-up ends of old straps and harness, ammunition boxes splintered and broken were strewn. I found the rope handle of one of these intact, and very hard I had to saw at it before I could get it off. Pretty good this, after three years of exposure to weather. On all sides were traces and remains of the flight ; here and there one would come upon significant heaps of earth or stones, or a rag of clothing fluttering on a bush just as it had been torn from some fugitive. After crossing the stream at the bottom of the valley the ground is open, but fearfully rough and stony, and so it continues the whole way. The bulk of those who fled must have been killed within the first couple of miles, according to the signs.

My companion had brought his gun, and a covey of partridges rising in front of us, he made a good right and left shot, dropping his brace ; but owing to the length and thickness of the grass, we could only find one of the birds, after much searching. Then we put up three or four bucks, which, however, kept religiously out of shot range, and we had no rifle ; so the mission larder was defrauded again.

At length we reach the brow of the last steep, and scramble down its rugged side. It is appallingly hot, as the middle of a February day in South Africa can be, and we have taken two hours and a half to get here, for so stony is the ground that we have been obliged to lead the horses nearly the whole way. 'Fugitives' Drift,' strictly speaking, is not a 'drift' at all; probably no one ever rode through it before the event from which it takes its name, or ever will again. There is no gradual descent to the river, which at this point runs deep and wide, and is only got at by scrambling almost headlong down a high, crumbling bank. The crossing was made at the lower end of a long reach ; in the middle of the water is a large stone, to which Melvill was clinging when his gallant companion, deliberately throwing away his own life, turned back to help him. Let us picture the scene. The swift, swollen river flowing on with a sullen roar ; the high wooded banks, whose tangled undergrowth resounds with the song of birds, while ever and anon the long-drawn whistle of a flight of spreuws, their bright plumage flashing in the sun, echoes from an overhanging cliff. Opposite, a long ravine, its aloe-covered sides sleeping in the dim heat of the sultry midsummer day. Presently an approaching clamour — louder and louder, nearer and nearer—and a crowd of men comes pouring over the brow of yon slope in wildest confusion. Horses lose their footing on the rocky steep and roll over, falling upon their riders, and the dark forms of a thousand infuriated savages are bounding in and out among the demoralised mass, plying the deadly assegai ; blades gleam redly in the sun ; despairing death cries mingle with the triumphant howls of the maddened barbarians, and the cliffs, which, a moment before, had softly echoed the peaceful song of birds, now

throw back, in thunderous reverberation, volley
upon volley of ringing shots.

A few, however, have got clear of that frantic
crowd. Look at those two, especially, who are
riding as if they had something more than their
lives to save : and so they have—the honour of
their regiment—its Colours. A plunge—the water
rises in jets around them, the falling drops mingling
with the plash of leaden hail. Now they are
through—no—one has disappeared. See, the
other turns back. Why does he not keep on, the
bulk of the peril is over now? A few more steps
and he will be safe ; it is madness, deliberate madness, to throw away his life; he can do no good
by it ! Who shall say that all this and more—the
vision of home, a future career, a hundred hopes
and ambitions—does not flash across his mind at
this moment? But he is a Briton and a soldier ;
a comrade is in danger, and the Colours must be
saved ; his own life is as nothing in the balance.
Again he disappears in that turbid, boiling flood.
See, the bank is lined with dark eager forms ; puffs
of smoke issue from many a point—' ping,' ' ping,'
fall the vengeful bullets. Both are down. No,
they are up again, on the opposite shore, but they
have lost their horses and—the Colours. A frightful yell wakes the echoes from the surrounding
heights as the fierce foemen dash into the river,

like bloodhounds, in pursuit. The two heroes toil laboriously up a long ravine, but they are wounded and exhausted ; their fleet foes gain upon them ; a few hundred yards, a short struggle, and—another brilliant page has been added to the glowing annals of British deeds of arms. The two soldiers lie pierced through and through with many a wound, and the Colours are lost ; but they have done their best—their very best. And the current rolls on its course beneath the great overhanging silent cliffs, and at evening time the low of cattle wending down to drink, and the song and laughter of Zulu girls coming from a neighbouring kraal to fill their calabashes, are the only sounds that now wake these solitudes formerly rent by the din of fierce and deadly strife.

About five hundred yards from the river, near the upper end of the ravine, rest the two heroes, beneath a stone cross on which is recorded their names and the manner of their deaths.

Our way back lay through a long bushy valley to the left of the Fugitives' Track, returning from the river ; the heat was fearful, and our horses were in a perfect bath as they stepped lazily along. Presently something white lying among the grass catches my eye ; it is a human skull, large and well formed. How can it have come here, right out of the line of flight as we are ? Some poor

wretch who has perhaps crept away to die in
solitude. Truly the region round about Isandhlwana seems a very Golgotha.

But a reek of smoke rising above the bushes
points to habitation of some sort, and threading a
narrow path through some well cultivated mealie
fields, we ride up to a small kraal and dismount.
Two Zulus are sitting on the ground, one busy
polishing up the other's head-ring ; a vessel of water
is by his side and a flat piece of wood in the
operator's hand, and a few women and children
tumble out of the huts to peer at the ' abelúngu '
(white people). We throw ourselves on the grass
and proceed to enter into conversation with the
two men : the Zulu is a genial soul and enjoys
nothing so much as a regular good gossip ; moreover my companion was known to them. Cheery,
good-humoured fellows were these two, and chatted
away at a great rate, and presently, at a hint from
my companion, some ' tywala ' (native beer) was
brought us. Now this beverage, which is made of
' amabele,' a kind of millet, and sometimes of maize,
does not of necessity commend itself to the uninitiated palate ; but when the cupbearer is a big
Zulu woman, most scantily clad, who, previous to
handing the bowl containing the liquor, squats
down in front and takes a preliminary sip, the un-
travelled Briton might excusably decline to slake

his thirst under the circumstances, and suddenly discover that he is not so 'dry' as he fancied. But if haply he has toiled along for hours in the scorching atmosphere of the Buffalo valley on a February day he will, I trow, think better of it; anyhow, under our judicious handling the modicum of 'tywala' waxed smaller and beautifully less, until the bottom of the bowl became glaringly apparent. But whatever are the merits or demerits of this barbaric brew, there can be no doubt as to its refreshing properties in hot weather ; to appreciate it, you must be genuinely thirsty, for it is not at all the kind of stuff to drink in cold blood. It is a very safe 'tipple,' intoxication being only contingent on the absorption of a far greater quantity than any European would care to imbibe. The practice of taking a sip before handing the bowl to a guest, has, of course, its counterpart in that of mediæval civilisation ; no Zulu would think of omitting this form.

We lay there chatting for some time, the headring polishing going on the while. These headrings, worn by the married men only, are made of the dark gum of the mimosa, and when well kept shine like a newly blacked boot. They are about the thickness of a man's thumb, fitting close round the top of the head just above the forehead ; as a rule Zulus who wear the ring shave their heads.

The unmarried men let their hair grow naturally, as also do the girls, unlike the Natal natives, who twist and plait their wool into the most fantastic of patterns and devices. Shortly before marriage the Zulu women let the hair of the scalp grow, which, when long enough, is worked into a conical shape and anointed with red ochre till it shines and sparkles like mica. Rather a becoming arrangement is this topknot, doing away with the otherwise roundheaded ' niggerish ' appearance. The same holds good of the ring.

While I was remarking upon the friendliness of our entertainers, one of them rather took the gilt off the gingerbread by asking for sixpence. My companion pointed out to him that it was bad form to beg, especially before an ' inkos ' who had come all the way from England to see them, and the delinquent tried hard to appear ashamed of himself. However, I told him he must come and pay me a visit at the waggon, next day if possible, and we could have a big talk, which he promised to do, and as the sun was low and it was cool again we started, parting from our entertainers with mutual goodwill. It was dusk when we got back to the Mission, healthily tired after the day's proceedings. Next morning my Zulu friend, who answered to the name of Jojo, appeared in due course. I found he belonged to the Udhloko regiment, and had fought at Rorke's Drift, and was well posted up in the whole question of the war. We had a long talk, after which I handed him over to my 'boys' to be well fed, and having stowed away his full share of mealie-meal and sundry jorums of black coffee— to which invigorating decoction, by the way, the natives are very partial—my visitor took his leave, hugely complacent in the acquisition of some 'gwai' [1] and sundry knicknacks dear to the barbaric heart.

Strolling up to the Mission shortly afterwards the first person I ran against was Master Jojo, who grinned significantly. I remarked casually to my companion of the day before, that that lighthearted savage had lost no time in looking me up, and had just made a pretty creditable feed. 'Why,' was the reply, to my astonishment, 'he says he's starving, and hasn't had anything to eat to-day.' When tackled with such flagrant mendacity the rascal was not a whit disconcerted : only laughed, and said that having got a lot of good things out of one 'inkos' he thought he'd better come and see what he could get out of the other. The humbug ! A fine specimen was this fellow, tall, supple, and rather light coloured, with a handsome good-humoured face, but, I suspect, a great rogue.

[1] Tobacco or snuff.

I climbed to the summit of Isandhlwana, which ascent is neither long or perilous, being at the north end gradual and easy, albeit good exercise for wind and limb. From the top a good sweeping view is to be had, and the whole battlefield lies spread out beneath like a map.

I suppose that for many years relics of the conflict will keep on turning up—assegai heads, buttons, and such like ; here and there a bullet is to be found, and cartridge cases in plenty. Every now and then you come across a heap of these, and begin to speculate on how some poor fellow made a long stand for it on this particular spot until his ammunition failed. On closer inspection, however, the illusion is dispelled, for about eight out of ten of these cartridge cases have never been fired at all, as you may see by the unexploded cap and the marks of teeth where the enterprising savage has torn open the case to extract the powder and ball. I particularly noticed that none of these unexploded cases were to be found on the outskirts of the field, all there having been fired off; not until one got upon the site of the actual camp did they become plentiful, pointing, if anything, to the fact that the fight in camp was hand to hand, our men being rushed before they had time to fire many shots, whereas those forming the outer lines of defence would have had plenty. And the above circumstance seems to make against the idea that there was any failure of ammunition. The heavier missiles had also been emptied of their contents, and unexploded shells were plentiful enough ; a number of these had been collected at the Mission, some of them being put to such commonplace uses as door weights and even candlesticks, while others did duty as borders to little bits of garden patches.

A few tombstones have been erected, mostly just below the ' neck,' rather as memorials than as marking actual graves ; for, by the time the first burying party visited the place, the bodies, with very few exceptions, were past recognition. One of these exceptions was Captain George Shepstone, of the Natal Native Horse, whose grave is on the slope beneath the western precipice—a pretty sculptured cross enclosed by a low stone wall. A grass fire had blackened and laid bare the whole slope, but the flames had left untouched the grass inside the enclosure, which stood out, a green spot, with its white cross in the centre, against the surrounding blackness. But one monument is shared alike by all. Towering above the sad and fatal field, the lion-shaped Isandhlwana rears its rugged crest to the sky ; and, looking on that stern defiant frontlet keeping its silent watch for ever over our fallen countrymen, I could not but realise how grand a monumental stone Nature had provided, as though to shame the puny efforts of Art.

And Isandhlwana's stately crest its vigil aye will keep,
Guarding our brethren's peaceful rest, wrapt in their last long
    sleep;
Gigantic looms its rugged height crowned with a halo wreath,
As streams the pale moon's silver light o'er the weird plain
    beneath,
Or at the close of scorching day, bathed in the summer mist,
Those iron walls by slanting ray of fading sunlight kissed;
And the nightbird leaves his rocky nest with shrill and ghostly
    scream,
As sinks afar in the purpling west the twilight's last faint
    gleam.
When the deep thunder's angry tone peals through the blackened
    sky,
Vivid around that summit lone the flame-winged arrows fly,
And the storm wind with a frightened whirl scuds through the
    troubled air—
Seeming defiance back to hurl from his huge front'et bare,
There, in his towering grandeur piled, unmoved through calm
    and storm,
Majestic o'er the lonely wild reigns that stern lion-form.
And fitter monument ne'er crowned the fallen soldier's grave,
Oft upon blazoned folds unwound floating o'er land and wave,
Emblem of Britain's might renowned, here watching o'er her
    brave.[1]

[1] From a poem by the author, contributed to the *Natal Mercury* on the third anniversary of the battle.

CHAPTER V

THE scene of the Prince Imperial's death is about twenty miles from Isandhlwana as the crow flies, but by road nearly twice that distance; and having thoroughly ' done ' the great battlefield, and the oxen being considerably set up by their long rest, we inspanned early one morning and took the road for the Ityotyozi valley. The first halt was at St. Augustine's, a mission station in charge of the Rev. Charles Johnson, about thirteen miles from Isandhlwana and four from Rorke's Drift; but a change of weather coming on, with violent thunderstorms and heavy showers, I was detained two or three days, which gave me an opportunity of seeing Hlubi, the chief of the district, whose residence is close to the station.

At the termination of hostilities there was an

impression abroad that Zululand was to be kept
for the Zulus exclusively, and that no part thereof
would be taken from them under any pretence
whatever : whether a statement to that effect was
made by authority, my memory does not serve.
Anyhow, a large slice of the country was given to
this Hlubi, who is not a Zulu at all, but the head
of a clan of Basutos living within the borders of
Natal, who did good service on our side during the
war. Whether another way might not have been
found of rewarding a friend and ally than giving
him territory to which he could have had no claim,
may be a fair question ; but, on the other hand,
looking at the arrangement as simply one of policy,
there can be no doubt as to the advantage of
placing the district comprising the scene of the
one great Zulu triumph, under an alien devoted to
British interest. As a matter of fact the two
border districts, from the Blood River to the
Tugela mouth, are both ruled by chiefs whose
interests are unmistakably identical with our own.

A middle-aged man, rather stout, with an intelligent face, dressed in velveteen jacket, tweed
trousers, and flannel shirt, and with a general air of
native well-to-do-ness, such is the chief Hlubi. His
aspirations tend in the direction of comfort, for he
lives in a substantial stone house with a verandah,
and uses tables and chairs. Furthermore, he

drives his own trap, an American ' spider '—albeit
given to loading up the same rather inordinately :
for to drive seven full-grown persons in a vehicle
constructed to seat four, *is* inordinate loading up.
At the time of my arrival the chief was engaged in
presiding over a ' trial-at-law,' so after we had exchanged civilities, he left me to resume his judicial
seat. About fifty natives—Zulus and Basutos—were
squatted round in a circle, with the defendants,
six in number, in the centre ; the ' court' was held
in the open air, Hlubi being the only man who
affected a chair, the others sitting on the ground
tailor-fashion. There appeared to be ' counsel ' on
both sides : seeing, however, that three individuals
would be talking all at once, both loud and fast—
and can't a native talk—it struck me that the man
who would determine the rights and wrongs of the
case should be gifted with an extra judicial mind.
An *indaba*[1] of this kind will often last for days.
Once a native orator is on his legs (metaphorically,
for the discussion is generally carried on squatting)
it must be a very powerful diversion indeed that
will arrest the stream of talk and gesture—the
gesture denunciatory or explanatory, the gesture
deprecatory or exultant, all play an important
part in aboriginal speech-making. And yet no

---

[1] Palaver. The word is also used for conversation, ' news,' or any kind of talk.

one could brand that torrent of volubility with the
ignominious term 'jabber,' for there is a wonderful grace about this pantomimic illustration—the
grace and ease of a born orator—while the smooth,
even flow of words, no less than the readiness of
repartee, betokens a command of language which
our trained speakers might well envy. A native
is never at a loss ; never at a moment's hesitation
for an expression wherewith to convey his meaning : how poor and wanting in this respect is our
unmelodious English compared with his facile
tongue. But I suppose the man does not exist
who, once upon his legs, more dearly loves to hear
himself talk than the native of South Africa, be he
Zulu or Xosa, Tembu or Basuto, or be he who he
may.

In the trial I witnessed, the defendants were
charged with resisting some of Hlubi's police :
whether they were convicted or not I never heard.

Near St. Augustine's is Sirayo's [1] old stronghold,
the scene of the first skirmish after the troops
crossed into Zululand, and this I took occasion to
visit. About an hour's ride brought us through
the green valley of the Bashi, and after several

---

[1] Zulus cannot sound the letter 'r,' pronouncing it as 'h ;' yet in
their language it conveys something more than the ordinary sound of
'h,' more like 'ch' in the German word 'ich.' Thus it is pronounced
in 'Sirayo.' Sometimes they pronounce it 'l,' as in their coined word
'umbulele,' umbrella.

tedious *détours* to get round a mealie field or to avoid a deep donga, we entered the steep stony defile leading to the truculent old chieftain's former abode. The morning was dark and lowering, heavy clouds completely veiling the *krantzes* (cliffs) and hill tops, while a constant and insinuating drizzle did its level best to render life exceedingly uncomfortable for the ambitious explorer. The site of the kraal, which was easily found, is on a ridge, or rather spur, overlooking the approaches from the valley on either side; the cattle enclosure still stands, and is girt by a solid stone wall, around which, and thickly overgrown with tangled weeds, are the clay floors of the huts, being all that remain of the same. On the other side of the ravine, in the rear, rises a huge wall of frowning cliff, along whose face clouds were driving in misty scud, the crags looming out stern and forbidding in their shadowy dimness; and here, amid the stones and clefts, Sirayo's followers made a futile stand against the hated invader.

A temporary lull in the downpour enabled us to compass a fire and some breakfast, which imparted a surprisingly brighter tint to things in general. Previously, what with the early start and the long wet ride, I was rather weary, and felt strongly sympathetic towards Nature in her abhorrence of a vacuum, which combination of discomforts had set me wondering whether it was worth while going through so much to gain so little, as the charity boy is proverbially supposed to have said when he came to the end of the alphabet. The look-out, however, assumed a more cheerful hue after breakfast, and I was inclined to explore the rugged fastness in front, but the rain coming on again harder than ever, it was manifest that no good could be effected by slipping and tumbling about among slimy boulders and long wet grass ; accordingly, saddling up, we took the homeward track.

As soon as the weather fairly cleared we started, and halting for the night on the heights near Itelezi, descended early next morning into the Ityotyozi, a clear stream whose sandy bed winds through grassy bottoms, where the track was anything but plain. Owing to its winding course the river has to be crossed several times, which, the drifts being nearly all more or less bad, is not an advantage. I arrived at one of these to find the waggon sticking fast, and the driver endeavouring, with a persistency worthy of a better cause, to upset the same. However, I was just in time to save its centre of gravity and avert the catastrophe, and after plying spade and pick for a few minutes, the offending wheel rolled reluctantly out of the hole, and we were on the move again. The next event came in the shape of a big puff adder lying in the middle of the road, which Fani deftly slew with his long whip, looking hugely pleased with himself after the successful accomplishment of this feat. In fact he soon got hold of the idea that the destruction of all the snakes in Zululand was his particular mission, and, thereafter, whenever a serpent showed itself anywhere near our line of march, he effectually 'did for' that unwary reptile.

The surrounding country was green and un-dulating, and did not seem thickly populated, though a few kraals were scattered about here and there upon the plains. During the mid-day halt some Zulus paid me a visit at the waggon; the gift of a little tobacco (which is not used for smoking, but converted into snuff), and a few trifles, placed us at once on the best of terms, and they sat chatting away about the war and their own politics of the day as familiarly as if we had known each other all our lives.

Snuff-taking, by the way, constitutes an eventful item in the Zulu day's doings. It is in no wise to be engaged in lightly or hurried over, but must be attended with all the deliberate ceremonial which so important an undertaking demands. Is the would-be snuffer on his travels,— he does not take his 'pinch' while walking along. Oh no! He sits down by the roadside, gravely extracts his snuffbox (either a bit of reed or a long tube of polished horn with a stopper) from the slit in the lobe of his ear where it is generally kept—I suppose because pockets are unknown conveniences to people the bulk of whose clothing consists of Nature's garb—pours a quantity of its contents into his bone snuff-spoon, if he has one, or into the hollow of his hand if he has not, and by a series of 'pinches' transfers every particle of the pungent mixture to his nasal cavities. Which operation completed, he sits for a few minutes in placid enjoyment of the results of his favourite indulgence; then, replacing his snuffbox in its auricular repository, starts on his way with the air of a man who has satisfactorily discharged a heavy responsibility towards himself and society at large. Three or four old men taking snuff together is a sight worth witnessing. The calm gravity, the sublime indifference to all earthly things depicted on each countenance during the operation is a study in itself. The use of snuff is not confined to age or sex, the women indeed being as fond of it as their lords; but the Zulus have never taken to the pipe, though the Kafirs on the Cape frontier, men and women alike, smoke ferociously, as do also many of the Natal natives.

But to return to our visitors. My field glass was a great source of diversion: they couldn't understand how their own kraal, about a mile off, could be brought by its means within a few yards ; nor how, on reversing the glass, the same object should appear far away on the horizon. But the climax of astonishment was reached when, unscrewing one of the ends, I used it as a burning glass and ignited paper and dry grass, finishing by lighting my long pipe therewith. One venturesome spirit went so far as to put his hand under the lens after some persuasion, but promptly saw good and sufficient reasons for withdrawing it, whereat the others laughed him to scorn. Nevertheless they shook their heads and thought that the man who could bring down fire from the sun to light his pipe with must be very big ' tagati '[1] indeed.

I arrived on the scene of the Prince's death at sundown. An old man who was driving cattle pointed out the spot, for the stone itself, being in a hollow, is not visible until you are right upon it. We outspanned about 500 yards from the enclosure, and almost before the oxen were clear of their yokes received a visit from the petty chief Sabuza and a few of his followers—it was on the site of this worthy's former kraal that the unfortunate Prince and his party were offsaddled

[1] Sorcerer, or anything that is uncanny, corresponding to the North American Indian term ' great medicine.'

when attacked. Sabuza is a quiet, good-humoured looking old customer, of sturdy build, and grey-headed, but an inveterate ' beggar ' withal. I opened the proceedings by distributing ' gwai ' (tobacco), and the Zulus, squatting down, prepared for a talk.

'What had I got to sell?' they were anxious to know. I explained that I was not a trader, but had come up there to see them and their country, and wanted to have a look at the Prince's monument. With a keen eye to the main chance, Sabuza struck in that he expected people to pay for the latter privilege, a notion which met with huge ridicule from me. The old man was evidently sensible of the *prestige* attaching to himself and his neighbourhood by the possession of such a ' lion,' and was resolved to make the most of it. I asked him if he kept the place in good order. ' Yes, he had told the white *inkosi*[1] that he would, and he did.' After some more talk they left, saying that it was late, and promising to return in the morning. Soon after their departure I strolled over to the monument. There it stood, white and calm in the moonlight ; every word graven upon the cross as plainly readable as in broad daytime. I stepped within the silent

[1] Major Stabb and Colonel Bowker, on the occasion of the unveiling of the monument.

enclosure; all around spoke of stillness and peace, as though I were standing on holy ground. And Ityotyozi's limpid waters rippled on over their sandy bed, blending in tuneful murmur with the rustle of long grass ever and anon stirred by a faint zephyr; blackly loomed the hills against the starlit sky, while a full moon hanging above in the clear vault of night shed a flood of silver radiance upon this quiet vale, where a promising life was laid low and the destiny of a great empire diverted. As I turned to leave the place a light twinkled redly forth from the dark hill side across the valley, and the sound of distant voices and laughter borne upon the night air seemed to bring one back to the everyday world.

In the morning Sabuza duly put in an appearance; others came up in twos and threes, among them my cattle-driving friend of the previous evening, who rejoiced in the name of Mpunhla, bringing with him some green mealies culled for my special benefit. I have said that the old chief was an inveterate beggar; the reader will judge whether he sustained that character when I say there was hardly a thing that he didn't ask for. He opened fire at once, first insinuating that I ought to give him a blanket, then ventured to suggest that a suit of clothes would add generally to his personal appearance. I replied that if there

was one reason more than another why I should
have elected to be born a Zulu, that reason would
be to avoid the necessity of wearing clothes in
such weather as we were then experiencing.
'Wouldn't I give him a shirt?'—'No; I didn't
carry articles of clothing to give away, they took
up too much room in the waggon.' He came
down in his demands at last to—a needle and
thread, but I was obdurate; as long as he went
on begging he should get nothing.   However,
I distributed some strips of coloured calico among
the assembly, which they proceeded to tie round
their heads with unconcealed satisfaction. The
amount of gratification which, in Zululand, can
be evoked by the bestowal of a few of the veriest
trifles is refreshing to witness. A couple of inches
of ordinary Boer tobacco places you on the
friendliest footing with the average Zulu; give him
a red handkerchief and he is happy; if you throw
in a few brass buttons his countenance will beam
with delight, while the donation of a coloured
umbrella, the gaudier the better, will make him
your debtor for life. I have more than once seen
a burly barbarian, in all the scantiness of his native
costume, striding along, as proud as Punch, beneath
a big umbrella striped with more than the colours
of the rainbow, and looking down from his fancied

elevation upon his less fortunate brethren who were without the coveted 'shelter-stick.' Lucifer matches, too, are greatly prized, being almost unknown except in the vicinity of a trading store. The native way of kindling a fire is by the friction of two bits of stick. A small hole is made in the side of one, into which the pointed end of the other is inserted and twirled quickly round between the hands until it smoulders and ignites the tinder.

In company with Sabuza and two or three of his men I explored the scene of the catastrophe. Looking up the Ityotyozi valley, on the left is a long bare range beginning with the Mihlungwane, two round-headed green hills. On the right the ground slopes gradually down to the river, around which are fertile low-lying bottoms planted over with mealie fields ; one of these now covers the site of Sabuza's old kraal where the party was first attacked. About a quarter of an acre of ground is walled in, and there is a small inner enclosure some twenty ft. by twelve ft., within which, at the head of a kind of rough altar tomb of piled stones, stands the 'Queen's Cross' upon a pedestal hewn from a solid block of native marble. The original wreath placed around the cross by the expedition, though much faded, is still intact, and a few other

wreaths in more or less withered condition lay
about.   The inscription, which I first read in the
moonlight, runs in this wise :—

THIS
CROSS IS
ERECTED
BY
QUEEN VICTORIA
IN AFFECTIONATE REMEMBRANCE OF
NAPOLEON   EUGENE   LOUIS
JEAN   JOSEPH
PRINCE IMPERIAL

TO MARK
THE SPOT
WHERE WHILE
ASSISTING
IN A
RECONNAISSANCE
WITH THE
BRITISH
TROOPS
ON THE
1ST JUNE
1879
HE WAS
ATTACKED
BY A PARTY
OF ZULUS
AND FELL
WITH HIS
FACE TO THE
FOE

'With his face to the foe.'   And now that the
red tide of war has rolled back from the land,

that foe so merciless and unsparing in battle is foremost in honouring his memory. Fronting the entrance of the enclosure a plank stands upright in the ground on which is fixed a curiously wrought brass crucifix, bearing a dedicatory legend. The graves of the troopers of Bettington's Horse are behind the cross, and in the left-hand corner of the enclosure stands the original rough wooden tablet erected by the Royal Scots Fusiliers; the trees planted by the expedition are growing up, and the place is kept in wonderfully good order. It will be remembered that the monument was formally handed over by Major Stabb, the commander of the expedition, to Sabuza and his clan, who promised to take care of it, and right well has the old chief kept his word. When we entered the enclosure the Zulus stood for a moment, one after another, and raising the right hand above the head, gave the salute of honour—'Inkos!' which ceremony they told me was always gone through whenever they had occasion to visit the place. A graceful and kindly tribute this, to the memory of a fallen enemy. Who shall say that a fund of generosity does not lurk in the breasts of these dark children of the wilds, whom we are accustomed to look upon as a set of brutal, inhuman barbarians?

I was at some pains to get at the facts of the

whole affair, which, according to the story of
Sabuza and his followers, were these. The Zulus
who surprised the Prince numbered sixty men
belonging to the Ngobamakosi, Umbonambi, and
Nokenke regiments—a scouting party, in fact. The
presence of white men was reported by one of the
number, who, from a peak overlooking the valley,
directly opposite the scene of the catastrophe, had
seen the Prince's party offsaddle at the kraal.
Thereupon the whole body moved stealthily down
a deep donga opening into the Ityotyozi; gaining
the river they crept along beneath its high banks,
and advanced upon the unsuspecting group under
cover of the standing corn. Those fatal ten
minutes! But for that disastrous delay the Prince
would have been alive now. The savages were
scarcely in position when the word was given to
mount, but fearing lest their prey should escape
them after all, they made the attack. A hurried
volley; a wild shout; and the rout was complete.
One of the troopers was unable to mount his horse,
that of the other was shot; but the Prince still had
hold of his—a large grey—which plunged and
reared, becoming quite unmanageable. ' We fired
again,' said my informant, ' and charged forward,
shouting " Usútu." The big horse broke away, and
ran after the other white men who were riding off
as fast as they could, round the slope. He fought

hard when we came up to him; the scuffle with the horse had brought him here (about 150 yards from where the attack was made). The first man to stab him was Xamanga; he belonged to the Umbonambi regiment, and was afterwards killed in the battle of Nodwengu.[1] We did not know at the time who the Prince really was, but thought he was an English *induna*. His sword was taken to Cetywayo.'

The bones of the trooper's horse were still lying near where that of the Prince broke away, but other traces of the sad affair were there none. Although at first blush it would seem that had the object of the party been to court surprise and attack, no better spot could have been chosen, yet the face of the country is so deceptive, having all the appearance of being open and devoid of cover, that those unacquainted with it might more readily be taken in. As a matter of fact, however, the long grass and numerous dongas afford ample cover for a lurking foe, who, taking advantage of the fields of standing corn and the winding bed of the river, could advance unseen upon almost any point, within an incredibly short space of time.

At the close of the day's proceedings old

---

[1] Or Ulundi. Zulus always call it the battle of Nodwengu, because fought nearest the kraal of that name.

Sabuza and his followers were rendered happy by sundry donations, and I made a speech on a small scale, saying I should tell the English *inkosi* how well the monument was being looked after, which announcement seemed greatly to please them. I told Sabuza that I wanted to leave at early dawn, and must have some one to pilot me into the main road to Isipezi, as the track was very indistinct and the country seamed with fissures. He, however, said he would go himself, and promised to be with me long before sunrise. But when morning came there was no sign of anyone ; so, not in the best of humours at being 'done,' I gave orders to inspan, wondering how the deuce we should manage to find the way, seeing that the grass was breast high and there was no semblance of a track. However, before we had gone many hundred yards Mpunhla put in an appearance, just in the nick of time, too, for we were already beginning to go wrong. He had seen me start, he said, and that none of the people were with me ; it was not good that an *inkos* should leave them without anyone to show him the road ; accordingly, he had come after me with that object, and lucky was it for me that he did. I took quite a fancy to the old fellow— so quiet and pleasant mannered, never asking for anything, but very pleased if any little trifle was given him. He told me that his fighting days were over, but I could not help thinking that he would have been a tough customer in his time, for he was a finely made man yet. How carefully he steered us through bad drifts and over the smoothest ground—walking alongside for miles, chatting and pointing out all the landmarks far and near, till, after two hours' travelling, we struck the road. When, lo and behold ! who should come trotting up but old Sabuza, trying to look as if he had piloted us all the way. The old humbug !

CHAPTER VI

The Upoko valley—A rencontre—Traders and trade—Mehlo-ka-zulu
—The biter bit—Zulu honesty—A Briton and his growl.

TOWARDS evening we began to descend into the Upoko
valley. Hitherto the country had been open and
treeless, now it became more rugged; large masses
of rock were littered about the undulating plains,
and a long bushy range of hills rose on the opposite
side of the valley. The open country, with its
rolling ' steppes ' of billowy grass tossing in the
breeze, has a certain charm of its own—even then
it must be seen with the sun upon it and the blue
sky overhead; on a wet or cloudy day the effect is
depressing in the extreme—but the bush country
is more pleasing to the eye and more alive with all
the varieties of bird, beast, and insect. Just as we
reached the bottom of the valley another waggon
appeared on the crest of the hill in front, which
turned out to be that of a trader. The rencontre
of a waggon in that wild country where for days
I had not seen the face of a compatriot was like

speaking a ship on the lonely sea. We exchanged civilities and agreed to outspan together and make a night of it.

The trader is quite an institution in Zululand, albeit there is but scope for an extremely limited number. Loading up his waggon with articles likely to be in request—such as blankets, knives, umbrellas, Salampore cloth (a kind of blue gauzy fabric much worn by the native women), tobacco, snuff, beads, &c., the man crosses the border. Perhaps he is fitted out by a storekeeper, in which case he gets a percentage on the profits, or the waggonload is entirely his own affair. He is away two, three, or four months, according to the number of his waggons, the success he meets with, or the route by which he travels. It is indispensable that he should be well acquainted with the native language; furthermore, he must be firm and businesslike in all his dealings, for the Zulu is a hard nail at a bargain, and will always try to get as much and give as little as he can. Hides, horns, and live cattle generally form the staple articles of barter; coin of the realm being scarce, and but little understood in Zululand. The habitual trader is well known to the chiefs, whom he takes care to propitiate with judicious gifts from time to time, an important item in the programme. He goes from kraal to kraal, living among the natives and

frequently on native fare. The best trader, too, is
the man who combines tact with courage and resolution. For, although a traveller may pass through
the length and breadth of the land, and meet with
nothing but kind and civil treatment, with the
trader the case is different; it is often considered
quite legitimate to overreach him if possible ; and
any potentate in whose bad books he happens to
figure may be inclined to make things warm for
him. The trip over, he returns to Natal, his waggon emptied of the goods he carried up with him,
but, in their place, loaded with hides, buckskins,
horns, a little ivory perhaps—anything that will
find a market in the colony—and driving along
with him a choice herd of sleek Zulu cattle. All
of which he disposes of, either to buy a fresh load
and start off again, or to return to his farm ; for
some combine trading with their ordinary farming
pursuits, taking a periodical trip into Zululand ;
others again do nothing else, having stores established in various parts of the country in addition to
their itinerary traffic.

While we were outspanning, I noticed a slight
stir among the ' boys,' the name ' Mehlo-ka-zulu '
passing from mouth to mouth. Looking up, I saw
a tall, clean-limbed native coming towards us,
swinging his kerrie as he moved through the grass
with an easy gliding run, two or three rough

lurcher-like mongrels at his heels. With the usual
greeting ' Saku bona ' [1] he sat down, panting after
his run, and began a brisk confabulation with the
trader. I looked with considerable interest at this
man, one of the principal factors in the bringing
on of the war. It may be worth while recapitu-
lating the circumstances. In July '78, six months
before the declaration of hostilities, one of Sirayo's
wives fled from her lord and master, and took
refuge in Natal. She was followed by a party
under the leadership of Mehlo-ka-zulu and Nkumbi-
ka-zulu, Sirayo's eldest and second sons, recaptured
in the Umsinga division, brought back into
Zululand, and there put to death according to
Zulu law and custom. The old chief appears to
have been unfortunate in his domestic relations,
for, shortly after this, another of his spouses suddenly preferred living in Natal. Again Mehlo-ka-
zulu came forward to vindicate the honour of his
father's house, and led another armed band across
the border ; the second recalcitrant wife was seized
and taken back to Zululand, where she met with
the same fate as the first. These little escapades,
however justifiable in Zulu eyes, were none the
less distinct violations of British territory, to
answer for which the persons of Sirayo's two sons
and one of his brothers were demanded by the High

---

[1] Literally ' I have seen you.'

Commissioner. Had they been given up it is difficult to see what punishment could have been meted
out to them ; the slaughter of the women in both
instances having taken place in Zululand was as
effectually beyond the cognisance of colonial courts
as if it had taken place in Siberia, no penalty being
provided by the criminal law of Natal for the
violation of territory. The war ended, Mehlo-
ka-zulu surrendered to the Secretary for Native
Affairs, and after a brief imprisonment at Maritzburg
was allowed to return home, as anyone who gave
the matter a moment's thought might have fore-
seen would be the case.

Mehlo-ka-zulu is a fine, well-made man, of about
five or six-and-twenty, with an intelligent face and
brisk, lively manner. A sub-chief of the Ngobamakosi regiment and a good shot, he is much
looked up to by his younger compatriots as a
spirited and daring warrior, but among traders
and border men he enjoys the reputation of being
an irreclaimable scamp, and many a bit of sharp
practice is laid to his account, of which the following story may serve as a specimen. I said that
Sirayo's residence, previous to the war, was within
a few miles of the border, over which at that time
horses and cattle took to straying in rather an
unaccountable manner, to be sent back with a
heavy claim from Sirayo for damages to mealie

gardens or something—frequently, too, never returning at all, and, rightly or wrongly, the old chieftain's enterprising sons were credited with these disappearances. Now it happened that a border farmer lost a horse which he at length ascertained to be at Sirayo's kraal. Knowing his man, he sent and offered Sirayo 1*l.* if he would find (?) the horse for him, to which the chief agreed. Time, however, slipped by and the animal was not forthcoming, but our friend Mehlo-ka-zulu was, and proceeded to inform the aggrieved colonist that his father thought 1*l.* too little ; they could not get the people to turn out for so small a consideration; and that he must give a lot of things in addition, among which blankets and ' squareface' (Hollands gin) figured largely. But while negotiations were in progress, one of the farmer's native servants contrived to let his master know that the missing quadruped was concealed just across the river close at hand. Of course he received instructions to go through quietly and take it, which feat being successfully accomplished, the naturally incensed settler turned upon Mehlo-ka-zulu, telling him that as he had promised Sirayo 1*l.* he would keep his word, but that he, Mehlo-ka-zulu, was an infernal scoundrel, and, for the rest, the sooner he took himself off the better. I believe there was nearly a battle royal on the spot between the two, but be that as it may, the wily savage must have returned to his ' native heath ' feeling wondrously small.

Whether growth in years, martial experiences, or subsequent intercourse with Europeans have diminished or eradicated scampish proclivities in this young warrior I am unable to say; one thing, though, I can say, which is that his reception of me when I visited him at his own kraal was all that was courteous and friendly. However sharp in his dealings the Zulu may be with trader or border resident, my experience of him as a traveller is all in his favour. More than once have I returned to the waggon, after leaving it alone and unprotected for some hours, to find several natives squatting round awaiting my return, pointing out to each other such of its contents as were visible, which contents they knew to consist of the very articles most prized by themselves, yet not a thing was touched. A fool, wasn't I, for making the experiment? Granted; but having made it, I like now to look back upon such an instance of spontaneous honesty on the part of these untaught barbarians towards a stranger alone in their midst, as if they had said, ' He trusts us and so he may.' If the fact of the Zulu being given to sharp practice, even at times bordering on rascality, in a bargain be cited as nullifying his other good qualities, I would simply ask if our own commercial mercury is exceptionally exalted.

I believe that, save in actual war time, any Englishman may go all over Zululand alone and unarmed with perfect safety, provided he is friendly and courteous towards the natives; in short, provided he behaves as a gentleman, and none more readily detect any flaw in such behaviour than they. But the ' Jack and " baas " ' [1] style of intercourse with the colonial natives does not go down among the Zulus, who, if treated with ordinary courtesy, are the last people to presume; at least such is my experience. Let this fact speak for itself. I travelled through the greater part of the country alone with my Natal ' boys,' and not one instance of distrust or hostility did I meet with.

To return to our camp. Bargaining was going on in a spirited manner, apparently, from the talking and gesticulation, and yards of Salampore cloth were being unrolled and measured, doubtless to deck the lithe figure of some swarthy nymph whom the chief's son contemplated adding to his sufficiently liberal allowance of spouses. I was anxious to enter into conversation with him when the ' deal ' should be over, but meanwhile was rummaging in my waggon for something or other.

---

[1] A Dutch word meaning ' master.'

On emerging thence I found he was gone, and could descry his dusky form disappearing in the fast falling shadows of evening—he probably elate at having got on the blind side of the trader, this worthy, on the other hand, chuckling over having ' made ' out of him. At the same time I am under the impression that in matters of ordinary trade—by ordinary trade I exclude fire-arms and liquor—the dealings are fair enough. If the trader gets a wide profit, it must be remembered that he undergoes considerable risk. His waggon may come to grief, his oxen may sicken and die, his servants may take it into their heads to desert him, and so on. Then, too, he has to bring the goods up there, and is working his waggon and oxen ; moreover, he has to feed his servants and pay them a high rate of wages, none the less so for ·accompanying him across the somewhat dreaded border. On the other hand, the articles in which he deals, though of small value in Natal, are greatly prized and sought after by the Zulus; wherefore a bargain which would border upon a swindle if effected in the colony, is fair enough in Zululand, taking into consideration the outlay and the risk. Added to which, both parties are thoroughly well able to look after their own interests.

These traders are a curious class, and my friend was not the least curious of them.   It was a glorious moonlight night, and as we sat over our fried rashers and black coffee, while our respective retinues fraternised round their fire—for be it ever so warm the natives always like a fire to sit round at night—he poured out his grievances. He had but a poor opinion of the Zulus as a people ; they were liars, thieves, and braggarts, and I would be sure to find it out before I had got much further. Once when his servants had all deserted him, they (the Zulus) had promised to find some one to replace them and drive his waggon, but instead of doing so had deliberately left him in the lurch. Then, again, they were always bragging about Isandhlwana; indeed, he had had a row with this very Mehlo-ka-zulu on that account. I ventured to remark that my experiences of them had been favourable hitherto, and that having had plenty of opportunities of pilfering from me, yet they had refrained from doing so.

'Oh, that was all very well, but if I were only to take stock of my goods and chattels I should miss a lot of things.'

I did not, however, miss anything, then or at any future time, but was ready to allow for the grievances of a man who probably had an uphill struggle for it in order to keep his family decently, for he told me he had a wife and four children in Natal. Doubtless, too, his experiences in Zulu traffic had not been all plain sailing ; furthermore, being an Englishman he must have his growl. We sat up chatting over our pipes till the moon was high overhead. When I awoke next morning my friend the trader was gone, and I could make out the white tent of his waggon moving along against the green hillside some distance off. He was not half a bad fellow at bottom, and I sincerely hope he may have many and many a successful trip under more favourable circumstances.

CHAPTER VII

An ' afternoon call '—Kraal etiquette—Zulu hospitality—Native mode
of slaughtering cattle—The story of a clever shot—Zulu opinion
of artillery—' Ubaïn-baï '—Sirayo—General feeling with regard
to Cetywayo.

SIRAYO'S kraal lies, one of a group, on the banks of
the Upoko river, at the foot of a long round-topped
range of hills, and thither when the heat of the day
had somewhat abated did Andries and I take our
way.

Passing an old military camp, with its tent
marks and low crumbling earthwork, we crossed
the rocky bed of the stream. A couple of hundred
yards further we came upon a rather slovenly
collection of huts, and were received by the usual
pack of mongrels yapping around ; these having
been speedily and forcibly pacified I inquired for
the chief, and was told he was out but would be
back soon. As I did not want to miss seeing him,
I promised to call again in returning, and meanwhile adjourned to his son's kraal, which was only
a few hundred yards off. Here I was more fortu-

nate, as I found Mehlo-ka-zulu at home. He was seated against the fence of the cattle kraal under the shade of a dried bullock hide fixed on a couple of sticks above his head, and as we came up, the barking of curs brought a number of faces belonging to women and children to the doors of the huts, to have a peep at ' umlúngu ' (the white man), a somewhat rare animal in those parts. Dismounting I walked up to Mehlo-ka-zulu, and took a seat on the ground by his side. ' Saku bona !' said he, with a pleased smile, evidently recognising me from our meeting the evening before. I replied in due form, and began to start a conversation.

On visiting a kraal the etiquette observed is as follows. You ride up ; the chief man, or anyone else who receives you, looks you up and down for a few moments and then greets you with ' Saku bona' (literally ' I have seen you '), to which you reply ' Yeh bo ' (Yes, indeed). He either asks you to come into a hut then, or when you have stated your business. The first question is nearly always, ' Where do you come from ? ' It is contrary to etiquette to go into anyone's hut armed or to hold a weapon in your hand while talking ; wherefore, if you have a gun with you, you leave it outside, or if the conversation is held in the open air you put it down. The meaning of which is, of course, that sitting with a weapon in your hand implies distrust of your host. It is also considered bad manners to go into or out of a hut backwards, or to stop when half way through the door and go out again. When food or drink is offered you it is always tasted first by your entertainer or some one belonging to him ; you may, however, decline it without giving offence, provided of course you do not manifest any sign of disgust with regard to its preparation, or the preliminary sip, if of a fastidious turn. It is sufficient to say you have only just broken your fast, or have not acquired a liking for sour milk or ' tywala,' or any reasonable excuse will do. On taking your leave you say, ' Hlala gahlé ' (' Rest quietly,' or ' nicely '), to which they reply ' Yeh bo, hamba gahlé ' (' Yes, indeed ; go quietly '). I used generally to shake hands with the chief men on arrival at a kraal ; it pleased them immensely and placed matters on a friendly footing at once.

When we had talked a little, Mehlo-ka-zulu rising, proposed that we should adjourn to his hut. Now my experience of the domicile of the Cape frontier Kafir—its greasiness, smoke, and squalor— I had not yet been into a Zulu hut—prompted me instinctively to decline the proffered hospitality, saying it was cooler outside : a shocking fiction, for it was something more than broiling as I sat there, nor was the bullock's skin large enough to

shelter me too. It wouldn't do, however, I was
evidently expected to comply ; so, going on all
fours, crept through the aperture with the best
grace I could muster. Once inside I was agreeably
surprised ; instead of the 'fugginess' and grease
I had been resigning myself to, the atmosphere
was delightfully cool after the fierce heat of the
summer afternoon ; the hard clay floor was beautifully polished and everything scrupulously clean.
A few mats lay about, and blankets rolled neatly
up and placed on one side. Several dangerous
looking assegais and kerries were arranged upon a
rack, while a ' mútya' of leopard skin, denoting the
rank of its wearer as a chief's son and a warrior of
some standing, hung from a peg.

The ' mútya' is a kind of small square apron
worn by every Zulu, and generally constituting
his sole attire. Suspended from the loins it is in
two pieces, the one in front ordinarily made of
Zanzibar cats' tails, the other consisting of a bit of
square hide, or in the case of chiefs and men of
rank, of leopard skin. This last, however, is worn
as part of the regimental dress in actual war time
or on the occasion of a review, at other times the
ordinary bit of hide. In cold weather—and it
can be cold in those parts during the winter
months or during a spell of rains, as I have already
found occasion to show—the Zulu wraps himself in

an ample green woollen blanket, for, though hardy by constitution, he can shiver at times, and, more- over, is not indifferent to the comforts of a bright fire and a warm hut while the biting wind howls outside.

The Zulu hut is a dome-shaped structure made of dry grass woven into thatch and stretched upon a framework of sticks, the outside being usually covered with grass mats. The floor is of hard clay, and, being continually polished with smooth round stones, shines like glass ; a small hollow in the centre constitutes the fireplace, and one or more poles, according to the size of the hut, support the roof. The structure is entered by a small arched aperture, just large enough to enable a man to crawl through on all fours, in front of which is a palisade, or rather screen, of mat or wattle ; the original idea of so small an entrance way being that of protec- tion against wild beasts.

Handing me a wooden 'pillow' [1] for a seat, Mehlo-ka-zulu threw himself upon a mat and settled himself comfortably for a talk. One of his wives brought in a large calabash of 'tywala' and a bucket of clear spring water : with the latter all the drinking vessels were carefully washed, then, frothing up a calabash about a pint and a half in

---

[1] The sleeper rests with his neck or cheek upon this implement, to avoid lying on or injuring his head-ring.

capacity, my host handed it to me after the usual courtesy sip, and filled a clay bowl for himself. Andries and two or three men who had dropped in making themselves happy with another jorum.

To my inquiries as to how he was getting on since the war, Mehlo-ka-zulu replied that it hadn't made much difference to him individually; his father had been a powerful chief but now was nobody, and had been driven out of his former country.   Still they managed to live.

'Did he regret having fought?'

'No, he couldn't exactly say that; he was a young man and wanted to prove himself a warrior. He had been in all the principal engagements: Isandhlwana, Kambúla, and Ulundi, and now he wanted to " sit still." '

'Always?'

'Well, that he couldn't say either; he liked a fight now and then; there was no mistake about it. As to whether he had killed many men at Isandhl-wana, he supposed he must have killed some one, but there was a great deal of confusion.'

Now this answer was evasive, for I subsequently heard that he had rather distinguished himself in the battle in question. As a rule, however, no Zulu will own to having actually killed anyone with his own hand, thinking such admission would be offensive; and so far from being ready to brag

about their successes, I invariably found the reverse
tendency to prevail; in fact, tough, wiry looking
warriors, just the most likely fellows to have played
the deuce among our ranks, are the very ones who
will most readily disclaim having killed anyone in
battle. Who shall say there is not something chival-
rous in this consideration for an enemy's feelings?

' Well, now, what did he think of Maritzburg?'

'Not much;' and, with a smile full of meaning,
' how easy it would have been for an *impi* to " eat
up " the place and kill everybody in it. They
could begin at Mkunkundhlovwane (Grey Town)
in the morning and finish with Mkunkundhlovu
(Maritzburg) in the evening.' In fact he had, previously to seeing it, pictured the capital to himself
as far larger and more imposing than it really was.

I told him I had just seen the place where the
Prince was killed.

' Yes, he remembered the affair, and was sorry
when he heard of it. That wasn't the way to kill
a man, to creep up to him in the grass and shoot
him. Zulus ought to meet their enemies in the
open, in fair fight, as they did us at Isandhlwana,
and at Kambúla, and again at Nodwengu; then so
much the worse for whoever was beaten, but the
way in which the Prince had been killed was not
good.'

There spoke the brave man and the warrior;

and certainly the genuineness of his enunciation seems borne out by the line of action practised by the Zulus throughout the campaign.

Presently a large piece of beef was brought in, which I was told it was intended I should take away with me, whereat Andries' eyes glistened as he thought of many a succulent stew to be concocted during the evening outspan. In fact it fed my retinue for several days, but did not look sufficiently inviting to tempt me, for the Zulus do not bleed their meat after the manner of English butchers, consequently it has a raw and uninviting appearance, even when done to a turn. The way in which they go to work is thus. The ox destined for slaughter is driven into the cattle kraal with several others ; a man then goes up to the doomed animal, and with one swift and sure stroke plunges an assegai into its heart—it falls, and they sit round until it has ceased to move, when the work of skinning and quartering begins. During which process, by the way, the Zulus do not show in a pleasant or prepossessing light ; indeed, a lot of them round a freshly slaughtered beast remind one of nothing so much as a herd of vultures. Sometimes the slaughterer makes a bad shot, missing the vital part, in which case the animal not unfrequently turns upon its would-be destroyer, promptly clearing the enclosure of all human occupants. I once saw a man thus 'chevvied' by a cow he had stabbed, and only escape being gored and seriously injured by sheer nimbleness and agility. Then they stood upon the wall and flung assegais at the hapless bovine, till they brought it down.

To return to my story. My entertainer was delighted with the gift of a red handkerchief to put on his head, and some strings of blue and white beads, which I afterwards saw him distributing among the ladies of his harem—he told me he had ten spouses—and as Sirayo had not returned, I suggested we should go to the waggon, and perhaps might find him there. Passing the old camp mentioned above, Mehlo-ka-zulu stopped, and began to 'spin a yarn.' When the troops were there a skirmish took place between them and some Zulus on the other side of the river; but what he wanted to tell me was that while a 'war-doctor' was performing his incantations there, a well-directed shell from the camp dropped into the middle of the group, cutting the luckless wizard clean in half.

He pointed out the spot, right away among the thorns, nearly a mile off; and to this day they believe that that shot was intended exclusively for the 'doctor's' benefit.

The Zulus have a very wholesome dread of the

effectiveness of 'Ubaïn-baï' (cannon). As this is the name by which artillery is known throughout the country, it may not be amiss to give the origin of the word, which is rather an amusing one.

Well, then, formerly at Maritzburg a gun was fired at 8 A.M., the hour when all native servants and labourers were expected to be at their work. After a while the time of gunfire was altered to 9, but 'Jack,' who has some idea of time, though none of punctuality, still persisted in sticking to the old hour, and from sheer force of habit would go to his master for his daily task. The 'baas,' however, would put him off: 'Don't bother me now, come *by-and-by*—when the gun fires!'

'What does he say?' would be the inquiry of an expectant group when their spokesman returned.

'He says, "Come *by-and-by*."'

Directly the expected detonation was heard, nearly every native throughout the city would exclaim 'Haow! Ubaïn-baï!' and betake himself to his work. The expression stuck, and forthwith the gun became 'Ubaïn-baï' among the native population of Natal, extending thence to Zululand. Some bold spirits have asserted that the expression owes its origin to the time that elapses between the report and the bursting of the shell. Not bad—but rather too deep and far-fetched an idea to take root so readily in the Zulu mind, and there is no doubt about the former being the real origin of the word.

Resuming our way, we soon came upon Sirayo and a few followers, sitting down in the grass. From what I had heard of the old chief—his deep-rooted hostility to us before the war, and his anti-English proclivities generally, I expected to see a grim, scowling savage; instead whereof, I beheld an urbane, jovial-looking old Zulu advancing to meet me with outstretched hand, and grinning from ear to ear. Looking at him I thought of the West African potentate, described as in full dress in a cocked hat and pair of spurs. His South African brother, however, was less aspiring, and rejoiced in a head-ring and a pair of boots (of course not omitting the inevitable 'mútya'), for the pedal extremities of this worthy were cased in a huge pair of bluchers, which, he being a great sufferer from gout, seemed about the worst line of adornment he could have struck out in. The old fellow lumbering along (he is enormously fat), with a barbed assegai in his hand, and trying to look as if he were not on hot bricks, cut a slightly ridiculous figure. It did not require much persuasion to induce him to turn back with us, and speedily the whole group was squatting in front of the waggon in high good humour.

I began by telling him I had been to look at his old home near Rorke's Drift.

' Yes,' he said, ' he had been turned out of his country, and was an outcast; a new chief, Hlubi, had been put in his place. He was an old man now, and couldn't go wandering about in search of new locations; all his cattle had been taken, and he was quite poor, and glad to live quietly where he could.'

' Did he know Mr. Johnson, the missionary ? '

' Oh, yes; Johnson used to be his friend, now he was Hlubi's friend, and Hlubi had driven him (Sirayo) out of his territory (the inference being plain). Why didn't we bring back Cetywayo? What could we want to keep him for? Had we killed him ? '

I explained that the King was well cared for in his captivity, but that as to the possibility of his restoration I could tell them nothing, being merely a private person.

' Well,' said he, ' give us back Cetywayo, and the country will be happy again ; or, anyhow, bring him so that we can only see that he is alive and well.'

Sirayo was always a crony of the King's, one of his most trusted *indunas* in fact; his son, Mehlo - ka - zulu, being also a great favourite. Wherever I went I found the same state of feeling ;

all the old chiefs loyally attached to the exiled King, and desiring his return. Always the same story : ' Bring us back the King ! ' This feeling is also shared by the bulk of the people ; and when ultimately I left the country it was with the impression that Cetywayo was that day the most popular man in Zululand.

After some more talk my visitors left, the chief and his son happy in the acquisition of a big knife apiece ; and a few trifles distributed among their followers sent me up like a rocket in their estimation. Poor old Sirayo, I could not help feeling sorry for him, though I am bound to say that his misfortunes were mainly brought upon his own head by his anything but immaculate conduct in general. But the war was over now, and resentment had had time to cool. An outcast, where formerly he had been powerful and respected ; his cattle gone ; one of his sons killed in battle ; an alien reigning in his stead ; his friend and benefactor a captive and an exile, and himself old, sick, and broken-down. Yes, I think one could afford to pity him.

CHAPTER VIII

A thunderstorm and a novel cistern—'Arrival of the mail'—A comfortable night—Matyana's kraal—Pastoral scene—The last new thing in shields.

A LONG night 'trek' brought us into the main road again, and at daybreak I started Andries off to fetch the post from Isandhlwana (for there is a post office agency at Rorke's Drift, and the mail, in the shape of a Zulu with a bag, runs to the Bishop's twice a week) about fifteen miles across country, and then, making a short march, crossed the Upoko, and outspanned to await his return, which would hardly be before nightfall. Opposite rose the cliffs and steep slopes of Isipezi mountain, and on the right the cone of Inhlabamakosi; beneath, a wild open valley, not a bush or tree to relieve the general air of desolation; a kraal or two, with its cultivated mealie patch, and a few cattle grazing around, were the only signs of life, and the oppressiveness of a dull leaden day seemed rather enhanced than dispelled by periodical showers of rain, which imparted a steamy dampness to the sultry atmosphere. Ever and anon from the westward came the muffled roar of distant thunder, and more and more distinctly, lurid gleams were forking amidst the inky blackness which hung like a pall over the far landscape. I could see that, unless the wind changed, we were in for a violent thunderstorm, which in these open regions, on an exposed hillside, with little or nothing to draw off the force of the lightning, is not exactly a joke. A brooding stillness had fallen upon everything till it seemed that you might have heard a whisper a mile off : the darkness spread, louder and louder rolled up each thunder-peal, nearer and more vivid flashed the lightning, and a spot or two of rain the size of a crownpiece warned that it was time to make all snug, and promptly ; for already the lightning was glinting weirdly along the huge dark *krantzes* (cliffs) of Isipezi, and fierce thunder tones sounded forth loud and menacing, echoing each long-drawn roll in a hundred rocky reverberations, to die away sullenly among the distant heights. Scarcely had we time to unhook the trek-chain and fasten down the sail of the waggon-tent when the storm burst in all its fury. Peal after peal in deafening succession ; steely, vivid flashes, almost scorching in their nearness, following so close upon each other that everything seemed fairly bathed in a sea of red and blue flame. Then a lull

—a few instants of deathly stillness, only broken
by the heavy patter of a rain-drop or two on the
waggon tent; it is dark as night, a silence that
may be felt. Crash! bang!—an appalling roar
—a dazzling sheetiness, and the ground reels. Has
the earth been suddenly cleft in twain? No, the
fluid has only struck something, probably a rock;
it was a near shave though, and I don't care how
few more such experiences I get. But the storm
seems to have exhausted its violence in that last
frightful crash, the thunderclaps, though frequent,
have lost *verve*, down comes the rain, literally in
spouts, the danger is over, and the storm-king
rushes off with sullen roar along the ridge.

And now I have to turn attention to more
commonplace matters, for the waggon tent evinces
an unworthy desire to emulate the distinctive
features of a well-ordered sieve; in plain English,
the canvas, having been so long dry, proceeds to
leak abominably. Basins, pannikins, mackin-
toshes, are all pressed into the service, but no—the
confounded thing breaks out in a fresh place, till
at last, sit where I will, a growing spout drops its
miserable trickle on to my longsuffering head.
Necessity, we are told, is the mother of invention,
wherefore, being blessed with two hats, I cave in
the crown of one which I cram on over the other,
and allow the water to trickle at its own sweet will

into the hollow thus formed. Fancy being driven
to making a cistern of your hat, and carrying the
said reservoir on your summit! But you are driven
into queer straits in the wilds. However, this did
not last long, the leakage ceasing as soon as the
canvas became fairly saturated.

Fani and Mlamvu, who have been sitting huddled
up in their blankets, stolidly waiting for the storm
to pass, now turn out, but it is raining steadily,
and seems likely so to continue throughout the
night; for there is not a break in the dull wrack
which envelopes the earth in its darkening shivery
folds, while the ground, which an hour ago was
hard as adamant, is now ankle deep in mire. No
chance of lighting a fire to-night, everything is
thoroughly saturated, so I turn in to the waggon
and make the best of it, which ends in my falling
off into a doze. Presently I wake up with a start.
It is pitch dark and raining heavily, the canvas
is lifted, and a round black head appears, bisected
by a double row of 'ivories' as its owner's mouth
expands into the broadest of grins. It is Andries
with the post. A good fellow that! Why should
he not, seeing what sort of a night it was going to
be, have turned snugly in at some kraal by the way-
side, and come on in the morning? I could not
have blamed him. But no—he knew I wanted the
post, so trudged on for hours through the rain

and darkness in order that I might get it as soon
as possible.   A good, faithful fellow!   And I sat
reading my letters by the dim light of a swinging
lantern in the waggon-tent, away in the wilds of
Zululand, pitchy darkness outside, and the rain
driving against the far from substantial shelter.
What a night it was; with one of those sudden
changes peculiar to the much belauded South
African climate, it had become horribly cold,
everything in the way of bedding was wet, so I
had to sleep in my clothes, in a half-sitting
posture.   Sleep did I say ?   Not much of that; it
was a case of shivering till dawn, and then a
' double' up and down the miry road to infuse
a little circulation into my benumbed limbs.

Towards mid-day, the ground having dried
somewhat, we were on the move again, traversing
a wide expanse of open plain; Ibabanango, a conical mountain, towering up, over a thousand feet,
on the left.   The day was cool, and the oxen
stepped out briskly. A few hours of steady travelling
brought us to the Umhlatusi : bumping down a
sudden and rough descent we crossed the river,
which at that point is easily fordable, and outspanned, but only for a short time, for the long
steep hill on the other side of the valley must be
left behind by nightfall, and the sun is beginning
to dip already.   High up on the mountain side we

pass the principal kraal of the chief, Matyana-ka-Mondisi, into which is being driven a herd of fine cattle, whose sleek hides glisten in the setting sun. It being late I give that worthy the go-by, otherwise should have stopped to have a talk with him. On reaching the brow of the ascent I look back. Great hills, now purple in the fast fading light, throw out their round, jutting spurs abruptly into the valley, the big kraal beneath is alive with animation, the shouts of the boys in the cattle enclosure mingling with the deep voices of its occupants, while now and again a resentful low rises above the rest as some recalcitrant beast finds its arrangements interfered with to suit those of its owners. Far below, the river winds through the valley like a streak of silver, and the grassy slopes beyond are specked with the dappled hides of many a herd wending its way to the kraals dotted about here and there; the shout and whistle of the drivers coming up clear upon the still air. And the roseate glow in the west grows fainter and fainter, melting into the purple and then the grey of an evening sky; stars peep forth; behind, the towering peak of Ibabanango fades into gathering gloom, and the hush of night sinks upon hill and valley. Passing along the summit of the lofty ridge we halt a little beyond Fort Evelyn.

From Fort Evelyn to Kwamagwaza the country

is hilly and broken, and the road in consequence
very winding. Far down on the northern side lies
the valley of the White Umfolosi and the Mahlabatini plain, the site of Ulundi and Nodwengu and
the other great kraals ; southward the wild broken
country stretches away to the Natal border, while
behind can be seen the distant head of Isandhlwana
peering up faint and blue on the horizon. A
pleasant landscape, open, sunny, and smiling. Herds
of cattle graze upon the hillsides, kraals are to be
seen everywhere, boldly perched upon a spur or
nestling in a sheltered valley, and mealie patches
show in greener contrast upon the sufficiently
verdant slopes ; for it is well watered is this fair
land, and the tall grass sways in billowy masses to
the breeze. No, there is nothing *mediocre* or tame
about the scene. The bold spurs fall abruptly in
sudden, well-nigh perpendicular slopes ; the
valleys, beginning in dark narrow ravines soon to
spread out and lose themselves in a broad smiling
plain, are picturesque with the fantastic dwelling-
places of their wild inhabitants ; and sharp outlines
of the mountain ranges, with here and there a
jagged peak, cleave the blue sky-line in the far
distance. Such is the panorama spread on either
side, as we sit in the shade of the waggon one fine
morning on ʼa high ridge some fourteen miles
beyond Fort Evelyn.

But the sound of deep voices and the rattle of assegai handles betoken new arrivals, and dropping their weapons in the grass, three tall Zulus stride up, and, with their open stately salute, ' Inkos,' raising the right hand above the head, squat themselves on the ground at my side. Let us look at my visitors. Two of them are middle-aged men from 5ft. 10 to 6ft. in height, broad and well-proportioned, their countenances straight-featured and bearded, with a good-humoured though dignified expression, and splendid foreheads, their shaven skulls encircled by the inevitable head-ring. The third, though taller, is inferior to the others in physique, but he is an *umfane*[1] and does not wear the ring.

Under the warming influence of a big pannikin of black coffee and some ' gwai ' (tobacco) wherewith to replenish the polished horn snuffboxes stuck through the lobes of their ears, my guests are in no wise loth to descant upon their martial experiences, or, indeed, upon any subject. The two first belong to the Undi corps, the youngster to the Ngobamakosi ; they had all fought at

---

[1] Boy. Among the Zulus, no matter what his age, every unmarried man is virtually a ' boy.' When he marries he is allowed to *tunga*, lit: ' sew ' (the head-ring) and is thenceforth a man. Since the removal of the marriage restrictions, a large number of the young men have thus *tunga*-ed, which they could not have done perhaps for years under the old military system.

Kambúla, and one of the older men at Rorke's Drift. The general opinion in the army, they said, was that Kambúla camp should have been carried, and certainly would have been, but that the regiments forming the outflanking sides, the Ngobama-kosi and Kandampemvu, were in such a hurry to begin that they got on too far ahead of the rest, thus affording the English an opportunity of routing and disheartening them before the main body came up.

'What did they think of the shells?'

'"Ubaïn-baï?"[1] "Haow!" Didn't like them at all. First the warriors tried to dodge them, and scattered when they saw them coming, till at last on one occasion when a lot had dispersed from where the missile was expected to fall, it astonished them by dropping right in the thick of the group that had just dodged it. Arms, and legs, and heads flew in every direction,' went on my informant, with an expressive gesture. 'This event caused them to lose heart more than anything, as they found they could not get out of the way of the "baïn-baï" so easily. At Sandhlwana the big guns hardly fired at all, and even then, when they did, they scarcely hit anyone.'

'But at Rorke's Drift—there were no big guns there, and the English could have stood

[1] See p. 148.

here (making my hand into a hollow) while the Zulus were everywhere; how is it you didn't make a better fight of it?'

'The soldiers were behind a *schaans* (breast-work), and,' added the narrator significantly, showing all his ivories, ' they were in a corner.'

' But at Nodwengu there was no *schaans*!'

'Then there were more big guns and more Englishmen,' was the reply; ' besides, the soldiers had bits of roof iron [1] which they held over their heads as shields.' I rather ridiculed this idea (one, by the way, that has gained implicit credence throughout Zululand—some even going so far as to assert that they heard their bullets rain upon the hypothetic bucklers), and pointed out the absurdity of a column taking the field, armed with bits of roof-iron.

' Did they ever pick up any of these things after a battle?'

But all I could say was of no use, the warriors only shook their heads as unconvinced as ever.

Then they began to talk about Cetywayo. ' Where was he?'

'Oh! he was all right,' I replied, ' and well taken care of;' at which they seemed pleased.

---

[1] The sheets of corrugated iron or zinc, with which most colonial houses are tiled.

'Were they attached to him? Was he a good
king?' I asked.

'Ehé! kakúlu' (yes; greatly)—this with emphasis; 'he was a good king, and beloved by all
the people.'

'Didn't he "eat up"[1] and kill a great many
people?'

'No; not many. A few were killed for *umtagati*
(witchcraft), but that was all right; if he (the
speaker) were guilty of *umtagati* he would deserve
to be killed too. Yes; Cetywayo was a good
king, and all the people were sorry he had been
taken away.'

I stood up and looked on the wide sweep of
rolling grassy slopes, over mountain and river,
valley and green plain sleeping in a glow of golden
sunshine, my visitors eyeing me narrowly. 'A
grand country!' I said, 'a grand country! "Sit
still"[2] and keep it; you've lost your king, don't
throw away your country too!'

'Yeh-bo!' (yes, indeed) they exclaimed, as the
idea seemed to strike them; then, rising, they
saluted as before, 'Inkos!' and gathering up their
assegais, started off upon their way. Looking after
their erect, well-knit figures, I could not but think

---

[1] Idiom for seizing anyone's cattle as fine or penalty.
[2] 'Sitting still' is the idiom for being at peace.

them fine fellows ; not a trace of resentment, no rankling bitterness towards their conquerors ; the war is a thing of the past, and themselves as cordial and open towards the stranger as though it had never been.

CHAPTER IX

Kwamagwaza—A desperate position and a tragic reminiscence—The soldiers' grave—The valley of the Umhlatusi.

THE mission station at Kwamagwaza occupies a pleasant position on the high ground overlooking the valley of the Umhlatusi. Tall blue gums stand in considerable profusion, being planted along the ridges and overshadowing the station, and on the steep slopes are large patches of cultivated land sown with mealies and ' amabele.' The huts are scattered about in clusters, with here and there an attempt at a square cottage, constructed of withes cemented with clay, and commonly known as ' wattle and daub ; ' a window, perhaps, and a rudely hung door finishing off the concern.

Kwamagwaza is a large station, but the people located thereon did not by any means strike me as representative Zulus ; indeed, there were Natal natives and some unmistakable half-castes : many of the tenements, too, were tumbledown and squalid in the extreme. The old mission building, as also the church, were in ruins, having been burnt by the Zulus during the war, which can hardly be wondered at, seeing that it would have been folly on their part to leave buildings which might be used against themselves, as was the case at Etshowe. The station is in charge of the Rev. R. Robertson, a veteran missionary long resident in Zululand. I attended one of the services, part of which was performed by a stalwart native cleric, who also led the singing with five hundred-lung power ; a good many people attended, the men being placed on one side of the room, the women on the other, and seemed to enter into the thing, the singing especially. Near Kwamagwaza are the graves of Lieutenant Scott-Douglas and Corporal Cotter, who met their deaths there under the following circumstances.

On the afternoon of July 1, 1879, Lieutenant Scott-Douglas and an orderly started from Fort Evelyn on despatch duty to Fort Marshall. Whether baffled by the darkness, overtaken by a mist, or compelled to leave the road for the purpose of evading stray parties of the enemy, nobody knows or ever will know ; anyhow, they missed the way, arriving at length at Kwamagwaza. There, it is supposed, they remained, hiding in the ruins of the mission buildings during the whole of the next day, owing to the vicinity of hostile bands. Let us imagine

the position of these unfortunate men.　Far from
human aid, in the heart of an unknown and savage
country ;　no friendly bush or rocks to conceal
their movements from the eagle glance of the
enemy's scouts, who from many a commanding
eminence would sweep the bare treeless hills and
valleys ; forced to lie close in the daytime, and at
night hardly daring to move lest they should lose
themselves yet more.　Only two—alone, lost and
without food—surrounded by ruthless foes with
the glance of the hawk and the movements of the
panther, what chance had they ?　On the morning
of the 3rd [1] they evidently tried to retrace their
steps, starting back by the way they had come, but
not to go far.　Cresting the ridge which runs right
across the station about half a mile from the ruins,
they were fated to fall in with a large body of
Zulus from the Empandhleni district who were on
their way to join the *impi* at Ulundi.　These immediately gave chase.　The doomed men fled for
about a mile along a spur, then, dismounting,
abandoned their horses and plunged into a deep
grassy ravine, presumably with the intention of
hiding.　Fatal move !—flight alone could have

---

[1] Subsequent inquiries proved beyond doubt that they met their
deaths, not on the 2nd, as was at first supposed, but on the 3rd ; for
the band that killed them did not reach Ulundi in time for the battle,
which took place on the 4th.　Had it left Kwamagwaza on the 3rd,
it could easily have done so.

saved them, for what possible chance had they of baffling by concealment those human bloodhounds trained in all the signs and sounds of the wilderness, able to track them by a displaced blade of grass or the disturbed note of a startled bird. On reaching the bottom of the valley they appear to have separated and taken different directions, for their bodies when discovered were lying some distance apart. I visited the spot where that of Lieutenant Scott-Douglas was found ; a deep narrow ravine, one side a smooth round slope, the other covered with mealies and tall grass, while through a line of tangled bush dotted with tree fern, plunging from rock to rock, a mountain stream hurled its clear waters down with a pleasant murmur ; and there, beneath the arching feathery fans of two spreading tree ferns, the unfortunate officer met his death. Standing there I could picture the whole scene. The desolate ravine, alive with grim dark figures and flashing spears glancing through the long grass—the hills echoing with exultant shouts as nearer and surer those pitiless savage warriors closed in upon their prey securely trapped in that lonely defile—and the doomed Briton at bay, his back to the hill, the branched canopy overhead and the bounding watercourse at his feet. Then the wild ' Usútu ' pealing in ferocious triumph—a sudden rush—and all is over. Whether exhausted and worn out by hunger and the hard despairing race for life, or in the hope that he would be spared, it does not appear that the unfortunate officer made much resistance. But that he died facing his relentless foes there can be no doubt.

It was a clear, still evening ; the shadows were already deepening in the valley, though the surrounding hilltops were gilded by the glow of sunset. I turned to leave the tragic spot, feeling that a kind of solemnity and awe pervaded it, as though faint voices from another world were mingling with the metallic ring of the mountain stream upon its stony bed and the weird piping of a bird in the sedges. Murmur on, winds, in the cool eventide ; fall, streamlet, with tuneful plunge into your rocky cells ; birds trill out your clear notes through this mournful solitude, this vale of death ; sing a requiem over the hapless stranger, done to death, despairing and exhausted, and alone in a far-off land—for these are the incidents that render war a horrible thing, rather than the stirring movements of a brilliant field, the fierce rush of battle and the din and clamour of conflicting hosts, the charge, and the ringing cheer of victory.

The remains of the two ill-fated ones rest beneath handsome tombstones erected by Sir G. H. Scott-Douglas, the lieutenant's father. Upon an eminence overlooking the sad spot stands the little cemetery—a square enclosure bounded by a sod wall, along whose top is an embryo hedge of aloes and Madagascar thorn. At the head of the tomb-stones still stand the wooden crosses erected by the troops when they performed the necessarily rough and ready sepulture of their fellow soldiers, and the whole is surrounded by a trench about seven feet by six, outside of which the ground is ploughed up for a width of several yards to guard against any possibility of injury to the place from grass fires. Three large cactus trees, visible from far and near upon the smooth hill top, mark the soldiers' burial ground, which, by a curious turn of fate, is also the old place of sepulture of a Zulu chieftain named Usidwa.

From Kwamagwaza the rolling open country continues; the road winds along over hill and ridge, commanding a view of the Umhlatusi valley, the river now and then glimpsed below like a silver streak, losing itself among the distant spurs, beyond which, in darker blue, the Indian Ocean contrasts with the paleness of the far horizon. On past the mission station of St. Paul's, down a nasty bit of road falling away from Inkwenkwe Hill, and we are in the bush country again. Huge forest trees rise above the mimosa and other bushes fringing the road, among whose gnarled limbs may here and there be descried a big nest of sticks, the

handiwork of one of the many species of large
birds of prey infesting these wilds, while creepers
and parasites hang in festoons from the branches.
Birds are flitting about, waking the depths of the
wood with lively call or note of alarm; monkeys
spring chattering from bough to bough; and
poised high over the tree tops, floats the form of a
rakish-looking falcon whirling in steady circles beneath the blue vault, his keen eye upon the noisy
feathered denizens of the thicket, while a suspicious
rustle in the tangled grass is heard as some big
snake, startled by the creaking of wheels, slips off
out of harm's way. Behind rises the high ground
we have just come down from, intersected by many
a gloomy gorge with densely wooded sides and
black overhanging cliffs—the home of the savage
leopard and prowling hyæna.

The Umhlatusi is a fine stream running in long
reaches over a gravelly bed; its banks, well lined
with reeds, are suggestive of crocodiles—of which,
in fact, the river has its full share in common with
all the larger rivers of Zululand; however, upon
that occasion we were not troubled by its saurian
inhabitants, who, under ordinary circumstances,
would fight shy of the noise and whip-cracking
attendant on the crossing of a waggon. They
generally prefer an easier method of circumventing

their prey, and woe to the hapless native who should chance to be swept off his legs when the river is at flood, or the unwary traveller thinking to enjoy a refreshing swim on that smooth surface. Calves and goats, and even children paddling too near those quiet-looking reed beds, have been seized, and dogs crossing the river sometimes disappear under their masters' very noses.

A grey scud working up across an already gloomy sky, and a few large raindrops, seemed to render a halt advisable before it got quite dark. With the exception of a slight shower or two, the rain kept off; but it was cloudy and lowering, and seated there upon the waggon box until a late hour, smoking my pipe and looking out into the blackness, the subdued crunch of the tired oxen mingling with the heavy breathing of my satellites, who, head tucked up in blanket, were sleeping the sleep of a good conscience, the effect was dismal in the extreme. For now the voices of the wild bush would lend their influences to the scene—the weird call of a night-bird, the yelping bark of a skulking jackal, the howl, or rather roar, of the large striped hyæna,[1] would ever and anon sound from the pitchy darkness around my encampment, while strange and 'uncanny' noises echoed from

[1] The 'wolf' of the South African colonist.

the ravines and caves of the adjacent hillside. A lonely and desolate place. Notwithstanding all of which exhilarating surroundings I was ready to sleep tolerably soundly by the time it became expedient to turn in, and the following day, cresting the southern heights of the valley, left the bush country behind and eventually reached Etshowe.

CHAPTER X

ETSHOWE, or, as it was originally written, Etkowe, is an open and commanding position on the brow of the heights overlooking the coast country. The first thing on arrival was to visit the old fort, which I accordingly did, accompanied by the Rev. Mr. Oftebro, the clergyman in charge of the Norwegian mission there, which is one of the oldest stations in the country.

The fort, then, consists of a substantial earthwork, enclosing a space of two acres and a half; it is oblong in shape, and surrounded by a ditch some 12 feet by 10. What with Gatlings and rocket tubes mounted at the corners of the earthwork, and the fosse staked and wired, the place was simply impregnable to a barbarous foe however intrepid, if unprovided with artillery. No fierce rushes such as whelmed the lines at Isandhl-

wana, and caused the fate of the Kambúla camp
to hang in the balance, could avail here; for even
in the event of the enemy's legions braving the
fearful storm of artillery and volley fire, and
surging up to the very walls, there was the gaping
ditch, wide and deep, with its threatening stakes
and wired network, and its kaponiers, whence a
few riflemen could play awful havoc among those
who thought to cross it.   No; the Zulus were wise
enough to see that the place was too much for
them, and refrained from attacking it; yet to
this day they regard it with a kind of satisfaction,
as a standing tribute to their prowess.

But although no open attack was attempted,
the fort and all that went on there was watched
day and night. Zulu scouts would creep up
within a few yards of the earthwork, close enough,
as one of them told me, to hear the *breathing* of
the sentry on guard, and our outlying vedettes
were more than once surprised by the lithe and
crafty savage, who, worming his way noiselessly
through the long grass, left the unpractised Briton
but a poor chance, as the following incident, told
me by a Zulu who had fought throughout the
campaign, may serve to show. This bold warrior,
then, in company with seven other congenial
spirits, were amusing themselves one day stalking
a couple of men on picket duty, who sat quite

unconcernedly while their deadly foes were advancing nearer and nearer upon them. ' While they were talking,' said my informant, ' we crept on ; when they were silent we lay still as if dead. We got within fifty yards of them, when others came up from the fort ; we did not like the look of these, so were obliged to go away again.' I venture to say that those two will never know what an escape they had. A peculiarly trying and perilous duty is this outlying guard ; a couple of men, or even more, placed by themselves, far from the lines and surrounded by tall grass through which the savages can crawl silently and with ease. Little is it then to be wondered at that the attacks upon vedettes were not always unsuccessful.

Imbombotyana, the high cone upon which the heliographing was carried on, overlooks the position, and another mode of aggression adopted by the Zulus was to fire upon the outposts from this eminence. But a party of our men, stealing a march on them in the night, got there first, and, lying in wait, opened an unexpected and effectual fire, mightily astonishing the enterprising barbarian, and completely spoiling his fun. Then the enemy· would playfully pull up the stakes which had been driven in at measured distances round the fort to facilitate accuracy of shooting in case of attack; a charge of dynamite, however, placed at the foot of one of them exploding with considerable damage, likewise put him out of conceit with this new entertainment.

But a more pressing danger stared the garrison in the face than anything threatened by the enemy. The season was a wet one, exceptionally so in fact, and here were close upon 1,500 men shut up within an area of a couple of acres, without shelter, and obliged to lie on the bare ground, which in the daytime was trodden into sloppy mire, at night reeking with pestilential exhalations. This could have but one result. Men began to sicken and die off, and on a steep slope in front of the fort a little cemetery tells its own tale. Beneath rough and simple, but in many instances tastefully devised, wooden crosses, twenty-eight men, rank and file, lie buried there, most of them, from the inscriptions, quite young men; and considering the bad and insufficient food, exposure to unusually wet weather, and the inevitable unwholesomeness attendant upon the circumstances, the wonder is that the death return was not much greater.

Looking at the fort now, one would think it had been constructed twelve years ago rather than three. Long grass trailing from the earthwork almost conceals the ditch, whose brink is, in

places, so overgrown with brambles and rank
herbage as to constitute a source of danger to
the unwary explorer ; the buildings within, that
did duty for storehouses and hospitals, are in a
tumbledown state ; in fact, the whole enclosed
space presents a woful and ruinous appearance.
At one end is a clump of blue gums, but the
fruit trees planted by the missionaries were cut
down with a view to clearing the ground in and
around the fortification.

I said that heliographic communication with
the border was carried on from the summit of
Imbombotyana, and no better point could have
been chosen, for it commands the whole of the
coast country. From the Etshowe side, Imbombotyana is rather an unimposing round-topped
eminence, but from its summit a splendid view
awaits, for the ground suddenly falls away a
thousand feet, and besides the low coast country,
which lies spread out like a map, the eye may
wander at will from the Tugela bluff to San Lucia
Bay ; from the broken mountains along the Natal
border to the Ingandhla range westward. Beneath,
a perfect picture is unfolded ; on every side hills
and mimosa-clad vales watered by many a silver
stream ; herds of cattle dot the slopes, and among
the symmetrical circular kraals may be seen
moving about the dark figures of their inhabitants,

whose voices and laughter are faintly borne upwards on the still air.   In the distance two
hump-like hills rising mark the site of the Gingindhlovu battlefield ; beyond, the ruins of Fort
Chelmsford ; and, like a speck, Dikileni, one of
the residences of the chief, John Dunn, stands
white against the plain, which rolls on till separated by a belt of yellow sand and a streak of
shining surf from the deep blue of the ocean.   A
floating haze, just sufficient to soften the golden
rays of a declining sun without impeding the
view, settles upon the landscape, and the scene is
a charming one.

Before leaving Etshowe I paid a visit to
Dabulamanzi, whose principal kraal is about six
miles off.   This worthy, whose name came greatly
into prominence before the war, is one of Cetywayo's
half-brothers.   Why he should have been made
so much of it is difficult to understand, seeing
that he is not an *induna* in any sense, and
whatever lustre may be reflected on him is solely
due to his relationship with royalty, except
that everyone, having got hold of the name of one
man of rank, was determined to make the most
thereof.   Accordingly, in Natal, Dabulamanzi was
forthwith constituted commander-in-chief of the
Zulu army, and its leader in every battle, quite
irrespective of such trivialities as time and place.

As a matter of fact he never held an actual command at all, though a sort of precedence was allowed him by virtue of his rank; the real commander-in-chief of the forces being Tyingwayo, in some instances Mnyamane accompanying to ' watch the proceedings' on behalf of the king.

Very picturesque are the kraals in the bush country, and that of Dabulamanzi has the advantage of situation thrown in, lying as it does at the foot of a range of round-topped hills, whose pleasant slopes are relieved at intervals by the dark forest trees of wooded ravines. Imagine two large parallel circles of thorn fence or palisade about seven feet high, the wide inner space being the cattle enclosure, that between them containing the dome-shaped huts. This one numbered fourteen or fifteen tenements, and rejoiced in the aspiring title of ' Ezulwini '—' in the Heavens.' It struck me as a rather amusing coincidence that his other kraal, down in the low-lying coast country, should be called ' Eziko '—' in the fire.' In the open country, where there is little or no bush, the kraals have but one enclosure, which is built of stones, and round this, outside, stand the huts.

We met some Zulus on the way, carrying shields and assegais; one of them was marked about the chest and shoulders as if he had been tattooed with Chinese white, which decoration, he said, was the result of a rocket burn at Isandhlwana. Two or three men were hanging about as I rode up, one of whom went to inform the chief of my arrival, presently returning to tell me to 'walk in,' which I did, metaphorically, and creeping through the low doorway stood in the presence of the doughty 'Divider of Waters.'[1] My lord looked decidedly cool and comfortable, squatting on a mat, without a rag of clothing but his *mútya*, and the inevitable head-ring encircling his shaven poll. Two of his sons, boys of about ten or eleven, stopped in their play to stare at *umlungu* (the white man) as I entered. One side of the hut was piled up with trunks; and heaps of rugs, topboots, brass candlesticks, lanterns, and other odds and ends were lying about, the whole suggestive of Isandhlwana loot.

Dabulamanzi is a fine-looking man of about thirty-five, stoutly built and large-limbed like most of his royal brethren. He is light in colour even for a Zulu, and has a high, intellectual forehead, clear eyes, and handsome regular features, with jet-black beard and moustache. But although a handsome face, it is not altogether a prepossessing one, for it wears a settled expression of insincerity and cunning which would cause you to have little doubt as to the deservedness of public opinion

[1] Meaning of ' Dabulamanzi.'

about him if you had heard it, and if you had not, readiness of belief when you should come to do so. That opinion I have heard expressed by those who knew the man, in two words, 'a blackguard.' With missionary and trader alike he is in disrepute, and many are the tales of sharp practice, if not down-right rascality, which were told me about him ; nor is he popular among his countrymen.

We shook hands, and sitting down opposite the chief, I produced a substantial piece of tobacco, which was promptly transferred to his side of the field. Then he told Andries to bring in my gun —which, in accordance with Zulu etiquette, I had left outside—as he wanted to look at it. He examined it with the air of a connoisseur (the fellow has the reputation of being a good shot), bringing it to his shoulder, trying the hammers, handling the weapon as if he could not bring him-self to part with it. I well knew what was coming, and sure enough soon it came.

' I must give him the gun.'

' No, no, that wouldn't do at all. I had the greater part of the country to go through yet, and what should I do without a gun? Besides, what would John Dunn, the great chief, say if I gave away arms in his territory?'[1] (which we were then in).

---

[1] Zulus are not allowed to possess firearms.

He resigned it with a sigh.   'Hadn't I brought him any clothes?'

'No, they took up too much room.'

'Or some gin?

'No, liquor was not allowed to be given away either, in John Dunn's district.' In short, the fellow was an arrant 'beggar'; to such an extent that during the rest of the trip his name passed into a standing joke and a byword among Andries and his fellows, who, when any of my visitors waxed importunate, would exclaim with emphasis, 'Haow! U Dabulamanzi!' meaning to say, 'Ah, there's Dabulamanzi!' or 'He must be Dabulamanzi!'

This practice of begging is by no means general among the Zulus, indeed I found it rather the exception than the rule. A good plan when you have to do with anyone of importunate fame is to try and 'outbeg' him; in a word, to meet every demand by a counter request, without the smallest compunction. But, as I said before, the practice is far from being universal, and where it prevails is an abominable nuisance, for you can't converse freely and comfortably with a man whom you well know to be all the time turning over in his own mind what he shall ask you for next.

However, in this instance I had brought my friend a few presents, and began by fishing out a white felt hat with a striped cord round it. This was accepted with a profusion of thanks, and he proceeded to stick it on his head, thereby metamorphosing himself from rather a fine-looking savage into a slouching ruffian—I never yet saw the Zulu whom a hat of any sort suited. Having sufficiently admired the effect in a looking-glass, he told one of his small boys to put it away, in the execution of which command I discerned, besides a lot of coats and trousers, two more new wide-awakes, and began to wish I had kept my 'tile' for the adornment and gratification of some more 'roofless' potentate.

A few further gifts met with ready acceptance, and then I thought my turn had come, so intimated that I was capable of appreciating a knob-kerrie.

'No, he hadn't got one.'

'Then what was that?' pointing to a bundle of sticks in a corner, among which I fancied I could detect a decent one.

'Oh, that wasn't a good one.'

'Good enough,' said I, on the principle of 'half a loaf,' 'and I wanted something whereby to remember my visit.'

Seeing that I was determined to have it, he sent one of the above mentioned urchins to clean it, and handed it over with great *empressement*. I have it to this day, together with better kerries —and worse.

We talked a good deal about the war and subsequent events, but I elicited nothing new in the
way of information or incident from Dabulamanzi,
who, like many other Zulus of rank, was reticent
in matters political to a degree bordering on the
suspicious—and after a couple of hours' *indaba*
(talk) I left him.

The word 'Etshowe' was a puzzler to the
British understanding when the place first became
notable. No one knew exactly how to write it,
still less to pronounce it. Some would write it
'Etshowe' or 'Echowa.' Others, again, would
make it 'Ekowe,' and when so written the chances
were a hundred to one that the British public
would thus pronounce it, to wit, with the 'k'
hard. The fact being that the word was originally
written by the Norwegian missionaries, who spelt
it 'Eǩowe,' the accent over the 'k' giving to that
letter the sound of 'tsh'; so the spelling which
most accurately conveys the pronunciation is
'Etshówe'—the last 'e' being short but sounded,
and to this I have adhered.

The derivation of the word is said to be this.
Coming up from the enervating heat of the low-
lying coast country and suddenly brought face to
face at this point with the fresh breezes that sweep
the high open regions, a native would exclaim, 'Eh!
Tshówe!' (an ejaculation of cold and shivering),

and wrap his blanket around him if he had one, or start off into a run if he had not. Such a meaning, though quaint and apparently far fetched, is nevertheless the probable one, for the first thing that strikes you with regard to the place is its bleak and windy situation.

CHAPTER XI

Battle of Inyezane—Scenery—An aggressive customer—Inyoni—A
trading store—Johan Colenbrander—A tussle, and a narrow escape
—Mangéte—Gingindhlovu—A ride across country, and a ducking.

IT was a glorious morning as we wound our way
down the military road, which, skirting the base of
Imbombotyana, zigzags along the ridges, and dip-
ping into a hollow, here and there, at length brings
you down into the bed of the Inyezane river. A
glorious morning, I say, for the newly risen sun
shone from a cloudless sky, and a curtain of mist
then lifting had studded the bushes with dewdrops
sparkling and flashing like myriads of diamonds.
Bright spreuws flitted among the thorns, sounding
their shrill but by no means discordant whistle,
and the air was musical with the low murmur of bees
winging in and out through the blossoming mimosas,
whose fragrant boughs, sweeping down over the
road, brushed the waggon tent as we passed under-
neath. But oh, how hot it was !—by the time we
had rounded the Ombane spur and crossed the

Inyezane drift, I was nearly baked as I sat on the box.

This was the scene of the engagement with Colonel Pearson's column on the memorable 22nd January, being, in fact, the first pitched battle of the campaign. While halted among the thorns the column was attacked by an *impi*, estimated at about four thousand strong, which after half an hour's severe skirmishing was routed with considerable loss. Though at first sight the circumstance of being attacked in the bush might seem to place the troops at a disadvantage, yet as a matter of fact it was not so; for the Zulus could not show to such imposing effect in point of numbers, nor could they employ their usual outflanking tactics with anything like such force as in the open. Hence the affair assumed the features of a skirmish, and while the thick bush did not prevent the artillery and rockets from operating with effect, it precluded the possibility of the sweeping and formidable Zulu charge, at the same time affording our men cover whence they could with coolness and accuracy pick off the enemy. This engagement is known to the Zulus as the battle of Ombane (not Inyezane), from the Ombane spur round the base of which it took place.

Beyond the Inyezane drift our way for miles lies over a plain, densely wooded in parts, in others open and park-like, sparsely inhabited too, for kraals are few and far between, nor are there cattle upon the meadow-like flats. Now and then a buck is to be seen standing on the outskirts of the bush, intently watching us ; birds of prey, too, are plentiful, from the small red falcon hovering over the grass to the huge crested buzzard soaring on dark spreading pinions above the tree tops. The Amatikulu, a clear stream with reedy banks, is crossed, and the dense bush closes up to the road, which becomes a regular jungle path, the trees in many places meeting overhead, their trunks lost in a tangled impenetrable mass of creepers and undergrowth. Strange looking trees, too, such as I had not met with before. One of them bore a fruit with a smooth rind about the size and colour of a shaddock, which Andries assured me was excellent, but on tasting it I found it bitter as gall. His palate and mine were evidently fashioned with differing ideas of ' excellence,' though from the face the rascal made when trying to devour it himself, I imagine it hardly suited him either.

Going along the bush road we disturbed the meditations of a large cobra, who thereupon showed fight. Again Fani was to the fore with his long whip ; buoyed with the recollection of like feats previously achieved he treated the elevated crest and flashing eyes, the inflated hood and sharp menacing hiss, with lofty disdain, and by a well directed ' whack ' put an end for ever to the truculent reptile's hopes and fears. Presently the country became more hilly and open, the domed thatches of huts glimpsed here and there among the bush betokened habitation again, and we passed several Zulu kraals, the sinking sun throwing a coppery gleam on the heads and shoulders of some of their habitants, who had turned out and were peering over their palisades to watch us go by. Halting for the night at the Umsundusi drift we arrived next morning after a short trek at the Inyoni river, a small stream whose mouth is a few miles north of that of the Tugela.

There is a trading store at the Inyoni, but it being Sunday, its occupant was yet between the sheets indulging in a late sleep ; travellers, however, are scarce in those parts, and it was not long before he turned out to do the honours. Curious places are these trading stores. Let the reader imagine a rough and ready building, divided into two or more partitions, round one of which runs a counter duly furnished with weights and scales. On shelves against the walls are arranged blankets, Salampore cloth, coloured handkerchiefs, rolls of tobacco, sheath knives, packages of beads, brass buttons, looking-glasses—everything in which the native mind delights ; while hanging from nails in the roof beams are buckets, tin pannikins, three-legged pots, cleavers, straps, hats, military surtouts, umbrellas, and so forth. One of the partitions, over and above its use for store purposes, will perhaps be fitted with a rough table and used as dining and sitting room, and if space be an object a mattress will be spread on the bales of goods which do duty as a sleeping bunk. At the Inyoni, however, things were on a larger scale, and the storekeeper had a sleeping apartment to himself.

Being Sunday the store is closed, and we sit in the shade smoking and discussing affairs in general. Presently the trampling of hoofs announces the approach of a party—two white men, and a native on horseback and leading spare horses. The new arrival is introduced to me as ' Mr. Colenbrander,' and I find myself shaking hands with a pleasant-looking man of about thirty, every inch the frontiersman, with dark beard and bronzed complexion, and dressed in buckskin suit, with riding boots and spurs ; a revolver in its holster is slung round him, and a formidable clasp knife hangs from his belt. The removal of his hat displays a deep scar over the temple several inches in length, pointing to what must have been a very awkward and dangerous wound ; it is in fact the result of a blow from a battleaxe received during an intertribal foray some months previously. Separated from his party, while pursuing the losing side, he was endeavouring to ride down a fugitive, who turned upon him and a severe hand to hand conflict ensued. The savage, expecting no quarter nor deigning to ask it, fought with all the reckless courage which characterises his race, and laid about him lustily with his axe, then driving an assegai into his adversary's head he strove with all his might to work it down into the brain; Colenbrander, however, seized his wrist, and for some moments thus they struggled. But the Zulu warrior, though a powerful man, was no match for the cool pluck and determination of the European, and, severely wounded in more places than one, Colenbrander succeeded at last in killing his antagonist, stabbing him to the heart with his own assegai. This encounter added not a little to the reputation for pluck and resolution which he already enjoyed.

Johan Colenbrander is of Batavian origin; during the war he served as a volunteer in the Corps of Guides with the coast column under General Crealock, and took part in the battle of Gingindhlovu. He is now established as a trader in Sibepu's country and is much trusted by that chief, to whose place, some 150 miles further north, he was journeying at the time of our meeting.

He is adviser and confidential agent to Sibepu, and a man of some importance in Zululand.

We rode over to Mangéte, John Dunn's principal residence, the following day. It lies in a hollow about two miles from the Tugela, and looks quite a village; besides the chief's own dwelling, a large comfortable-looking house with a verandah, there are other tenements great and small, including the 'office,' gaol, &c., and the quarters of his secretary, an Englishman. There is also a school, where a number of the chief's daughters are being educated under a European governess. Within a couple of miles is St. Andrew's Mission, one of Bishop McKenzie's stations; whereby it will appear that John Dunn is not averse to tolerating missionaries as such, though sternly (and rightly) excluding the *political* missionary from his territory.

On reaching Mangéte I learnt that the chief was not expected back for some time, being away at his other place in the Umgoye mountains, which was disappointing, as I wanted to make his acquaintance. Therefore when Colenbrander proposed that I should take a ride up there with him, as he was going that way, it seemed the very solution of the difficulty; accordingly, starting the waggon off on the backward track with orders to await my arrival at Etshowe, I strapped a mackintosh on to the saddle and was ready for a start.

A couple of hours' easy riding—for it was hot
—brought us to the Amatikulu, some twenty miles
below where I had previously crossed, and after
watering our horses in the clear stream we held on.
Passing Fort Crealock—formerly a strong earthwork but now deserted and in ruins, being, like all
the other ' forts ' built in the country, constructed
for purposes of temporary entrenchment only—on,
through fields of standing corn and pumpkin
patches, past a couple of shanties, where we halted
a few minutes while my companion exchanged
civilities and ' chaff' with some very rough specimens of Dutch humanity, and presently we turned
off the waggon track to visit the battlefield of
Gingindhlovu. As we rode slowly up the long
slope down which the horsemen charged the fleeing
Zulus, a white object glistening among the grass
attracted my attention. It was a single skull, and
a fine large head it must have belonged to ; no
bones were to be seen around, nor while exploring
the field did we find any other relics of the engagement—nothing but this one solitary skull.

Gingindhlovu struck me as one of the most God-
forsaken places I had ever seen. Standing within
the low crumbling earthwork I looked around.
To the north the ground stretched away for miles,
flat and open, dotted here and there with clumps
of bush, to where a range of hills shut in the

view ; on the left front the Ombane spur, above
and beyond which rises Imbombotyana.   From this
direction the attack was first made, the right horn
of the *impi* meanwhile, sweeping up on the other
side of the *laager*, succeeded, by reason of the lay
of the ground, in getting within two hundred yards
of the entrenchment before being discovered.   This
side was led by our friend Dabulamanzi on horseback, who, however, found it expedient to with-
draw, the riflemen making things altogether too
warm for him.   The attacking force has been
estimated at about eleven thousand, and was under
the command of Sigcwelegcwele, the *induna* of the
Ngobamakosi regiment—Dabulamanzi being also
there on his own account.   On the west side of
the earthwork lie buried the officers and men
who fell in the engagement, the grave of Colonel
Northey having a wooden cross over it painted
white.

The sky had become overcast, and as we turned
to leave the place great inky clouds were gathering
up over the mountains to northward, and the long
low boom of distant thunder was ever and anon
borne across the still waste.   When we had ridden
a little way I looked back—there stood the wooden
cross by the side of the crumbling earthwork,
gleaming white upon the bare dismal plain.   A
lonely grave in a strange and lonely spot.

We passed the ruins of the old Gingindhlovu [1] kraal, and soon arrived at Dikileni, John Dunn's halfway house, where we would offsaddle for an hour, then on again. Travelling rapidly over wide flat plains, we leave Fort Chelmsford away on our left, and the Umgoye range rises nearer and nearer in front; but the weather is threatening, and though only a few drops of rain have come near us, heavy showers are falling in the mountains ahead. The ground gets more uneven, and presently the rain comes down in earnest. Crossing the Umlalasi we are fairly among the mountains, winding in and out by narrow paths well known to my companion and saving a considerable distance. High round-topped hills, through whose grassy valleys rivulets are bounding, their courses marked by lines of tree ferns and yellow-wood, the bridle path carries us higher and higher, till at length we crest the last ridge and arrive amidst deluging torrents of rain at our destination.

[1] From 'Ginga,' 'roll,' in the sense of 'roll over,' and 'indhlovu,' 'the elephant.'

CHAPTER XII

A WILD and picturesque valley in the Umgoye
range, shut in by forest-clad hilltops and cleft by
a clear stream leaping from rock to rock in many
an eddying pool—on a spur overlooking this
stands Ncandúku,[1] the mountain residence of the
chief, John Dunn. A single-storeyed house, with
verandah on two sides, dining and sitting rooms,
and plenty of bedrooms—a more comfortable
dwelling than the generality of frontier houses,
even within the colonial border. At the back are
the stables (for the chief is particular in matters of
horseflesh), offices, and other outbuildings, while in
front a fruit garden slopes down to the stream. A
large circular kraal lies in a hollow just below the
house, and strips of cultivated land are laid out
along the river bed ; the place is well shaded, if

---

[1] Nca-indúku, 'hit a stick,' in the sense of parrying a blow.

anything rather too closed in with trees. Such is Ncandúku.

And now a word as to its owner, about whom I have from time to time been asked all manner of absurd questions, even by those whom one might have expected to know better. ' Didn't he wear the head-ring, or live in a hut, or dress in a blanket ? ' and so on. John Dunn is a handsome, well-built man, about five feet eight in height, with good forehead, regular features, and keen grey eyes ; a closely cut iron-grey beard hides the lower half of his bronzed, weather-tanned countenance, and a look of determination and shrewdness is discernible in every lineament. So far from affecting native costume, the chief was, if anything, more neatly dressed than the average colonist, in plain tweed suit and wideawake hat. In manner he is quiet and unassuming, and no trace of self-glorification or ' bounce ' is there about him. He has a reputation for reticence—a fault in the right direction by the way, for his part is a trying and difficult one, and the more uncommunicative he is the better—doubtless owing his success in great measure to the fact that he knows how and when to hold his tongue.

We met with a kind welcome, and towards dark sat down to a well served and plentiful spread, being waited on by a tall head-ringed man, who moved noiselessly about with an aptness that any civilised butler or club waiter might have envied. We turned in somewhat early, for the chief, besides being a man of temperate habits, is a practical believer in the ' early to bed, early to rise ' maxim, and the next morning Colenbrander and I parted company, he continuing his journey northward, and I remaining a day or two longer at Ncandúku. I declined his invitation to join him in a sea-cow shooting expedition in the winter, though if ever I did launch out into that particular branch of venerie, I should not wish for a better companion.

The territory under the sway of John Dunn lies between the Tugela and Umhlatusi rivers, and is about 100 miles in length, extending along the border to within fifteen miles of Isandhlwana, where it joins Hlubi's district. So far as I could judge, it appeared to be as orderly and well governed as that of any other potentate, and a great deal more so than those of some. Three European ' administrators ' or magistrates—one of these, by the way, being the son of Mr. Oftebro, the missionary at Etshowe—are stationed in different parts of the country, whose business is to collect hut tax and adjudicate upon petty cases, the more serious ones being decided by the chief himself, to whom of course lies the right of appeal in any. Offences capitally punishable, such as murder, are

1. Three Zulu headmen, photographed in the early 1880s, and much as Mitford might have seen them. They are wearing ceremonial regalia and carrying small personal shields, rather than the full-size war shields of the old Zulu army. (*Killie Campbell Collection*)

2. *(Left)* A young Zulu man in everyday costume, carrying a war shield and a finely shaped knobkerry. *(S. Bourquin)*

3. *(Right)* A Zulu man wearing his hair fashioned into a bizarre shape with clay and tallow, in a way which was popular amongst unmarried men in the 1870s and 80s. He is also wearing snuff spoons through the lobes of his ears, and snuff containers in his necklace. Mitford was not the only European traveller who noticed the Zulu fondness for snuff! *(S. Bourquin)*

4. An impressive study of a Zulu chief in full regalia, photographed at the turn of the century. His body is almost completely obscured by cow-tails dangling from his neck, arms and legs, and on either side of his head he wears bunches of the red and green feathers of the Lourie which, along with the indlendla staff in his right hand, are indicative of his rank. *(Local History Museum, Durban)*

5. The mission station at Rorke's Drift today. When Mitford visited th
the hospital destroyed in the fight: this building, in the centre of the pictu
barricades were built along the top of the ledge in the foreground.

e, he found the Reverend Witt rebuilding his house over the ruins of
till stands, and is now part of the on-site museum. The original British

6. Isandlwana: 'The Last Post'. A lone bugler plays a tribute to the fall

idst the monuments and cairns which commemorate the fighting today.

7. The Fugitives' Trail, along which the British survivors of Isandlwana fled after the battle, pursued by the Zulus, is seamed with gulleys and chasms where many came to grief. Mitford found them still littered with debris and the skeletons of horses.

8. (*Left*) The grave of Lieutenants Melvill and Coghill, overlooking Fugitives' Drift in the Mzinyathi valley. The grave was originally marked by a white stone cross erected in 1879 at the request of Sir Bartle Frere: in 1973 this cross was destroyed by vandals, and replaced by the present memorial.

9. (*Below*) The Prince Imperial's monument on the site of his death, which can have changed little since Mitford's day.

10. 'Through the Zulu country'

11. *(Left)* The graves of Lieutenant Scott Douglas and Corporal Cotter at Kwa Magwaza. The tombstones erected by Scott Douglas's father still stand, as Mitford saw them, and the spot is no less lovely now than a century ago.

12. *(Below)* The remains of Fort Pearson, the base of the Right Flank column of the British invasion force, can still be found on a knoll overlooking the lower drift on the Thukela river – the old Zulu border.

13. The palisades and overgrown trenches of Colonel Pearson's fort at Eshowe have scarcely changed since Mitford described them.

14. *(Above)* The battlefield memorial marking the site of Lord Chelmsford's square at Ulundi. Three years after the fight, Mitford found the scene one of desolation, with the remains of dead Zulus still lying in the bush. This monument was erected in 1943: today, archaeologists are restoring part of King Cetshwayo's old Ulundi homestead nearby.

15. *(Left)* 'Playing tourist': Ian Knight in Mitford's footsteps at the Natal Carbineer Memorial, Isandlwana.

16. The dizzying view from the summit Hlobane, the Zulu stronghold unsuccessfully attacked by the British in March 1879. The view down the 'Devil's Pass', where Buller's men descended to Ntendeka below, has hardly changed since Mitford described it so vividly.

17. *(Above)* The British cemetery at Khambula battlefield, on the slopes below the old camp, which lay on the crest of the rise in the background.

18. *(Below)* 'The tumbledown wall and crumbling earthwork of the fort still crests the mound': lower now than in 1882, but the remains of the redoubt are still visible at Khambula.

19. For anyone interested in following Mitford's travels, the Fugitives' Drift lodge, which lies within sight of both Isandlwana and the Shiyane hill at Rorke's Drift (in the distance on this photo) is an essential and atmospheric port of call.

tried before a full court, constituted of all the 'administrators' and native *indunas*, and presided over by the chief, who is very attentive to all matters connected with the administration of justice; he has an organised staff of native police under a white inspector, and is frequently occupied the whole day in hearing cases. The 'administrators' receive a fixed yearly salary from the chief.

A sore point with John Dunn was the possible restoration of Cetywayo, which he looked upon as a direct breach of faith with himself. It must be remembered that Sir Garnet Wolseley's words on the subject were explicit when addressing the chiefs and people at Ulundi on September 1, 1879. Said he, ' It is six years ago on this very day, September 1, that Cetywayo was crowned king of the Zulus, and only yesterday you yourselves saw him carried away a prisoner, never to return again to Zululand.' *Never to return again to Zululand*—and on that understanding, said John Dunn, he and the other chiefs undertook the responsibilities of the territories allotted to them. That was the basis of the Ulundi settlement, the perpetual exile of Cetywayo from Zululand ; and as long as the chiefs appointed under that settlement observed the provisions of their deed of appointment, it would be a monstrous breach of faith on the part of the Imperial Government to oust them.

A great many ungenerous things have been said and written about John Dunn, mainly attributable, I cannot but think, to jealousy of a man who has made a position for himself and is reputed wealthy. One of the commonest charges against him is that of supplying the Zulus with firearms previous to the war. Even if he did, was he alone in this? Further, would those who make the most outcry about it have refrained from doing likewise, given the chance? I doubt it greatly. And then one seems to remember hearing it pretty frequently laid down as an axiom, that the natives are more formidable when armed with their own weapon, the assegai, than with firearms. If this be so, how in the name of logic can anyone make a grievance of their possessing firearms which they are unable to use with precision, are likely to cumber their movements in the field, and, better still, cause them to deteriorate in and abandon the use of their own weapon?

Another reproach hurled at the chief is that he has become ' a regular Zulu ' and is a polygamist. If he prefers living in Zululand and occupying a high position among its people to living in Natal, a unit among his fellow-countrymen, it is purely his own affair: I can imagine a man who has led a wild, roving life finding the position of chief, among a brave and superior race like the Zulus, one not unworthy of his ambition. His domestic relations, again, are entirely his own concern ; he lives in Zululand, not in European society; he does not bring his wives with him when he visits the colony, nor on these occasions can anyone cite a single instance of his acting in a way unbecoming the usages of civilised society.

Persons wishing to trade in the territory are required to take out a licence, paying for the same at a fixed rate per waggon, but all trafficking in firearms or ardent spirits is strictly prohibited under any circumstances.

I emphatically assert that on the ground of his proscription of the liquor traffic alone, John Dunn is entitled to the thanks of all true philanthropists, and whatever may be his shortcomings in other respects, this would go far towards whitewashing them. Look at Kafirland and the locations along the Cape frontier, studded with canteens enjoying an almost unrestricted right of sale—and what is the state of the natives ? A thieving, filthy, impudent, worthless set of vagabonds, a pest to their unfortunate neighbourhoods, never reliable and always discontented, spending all their earnings in drink when they do condescend to work. I have seen as many as a hundred Kafirs round one of these canteens in a state of semi- and complete intoxication ; and there they sit and drink, working themselves into a sort of frenzy, till a word brings about a blow, and a savage fight ensues. Cape colonists complain that the Kafir becomes more worthless and impudent every day, and wonder thereat; yet not only the country but every border town swarms with canteens, their walls red with Kafir ochre.

Now let us turn to Zululand—and what a contrast! Here are no canteens, and instead of the slouching, drunken barbarian of the Cape border, you find the well-made, intellectual-looking Zulu, with his open greeting and cheery smile—a savage also, but a fine savage, cleanly in his person and dwelling, and honest withal, with whom, except in actual time of war, the traveller and his belongings may move about in safety, as I have already shown. And the time will come, as ' British influence' extends, when the country will be ' opened up,' the trading store and canteen run hand in hand, and the demoralisation of this splendid race will begin. Then we shall hear people talking of how the Zulus have ' deteriorated.' Therefore, in prohibiting the sale of intoxicating liquor in his territory, John Dunn is acting as a wise and far-seeing ruler, and really doing more for the welfare of his people than by building a legion of schools and churches.

He has been accused of tyranny and wholesale

' eating-up,' but it should be borne in mind that savages must be ruled with a strong hand, half measures being worse than none at all : further, that the leaders of the King's party, his relations and others, were sullenly and but passively acquiescent in the settlement of the country, as indeed they still are ; and if the chief was obliged to resort to occasional acts of severity in order to maintain his authority, there was every excuse for him. Added to this must be considered the exaggeration inseparable from nineteen out of twenty cases of the kind, and in about the same proportion to them. That of Sitimela is one in point.

About eighteen months ago, one Sitimela, by birth a Tonga, but hailing from Natal, set up a claim to the chieftainship of the Utetwa tribe, and further, to the throne of Zululand itself. Having collected a force, this ambitious gentleman made a descent upon the territory of Umlandela, a next door neighbour of John Dunn's, who forthwith fled to him for assistance. The intervention of Mr. Osborn, the British resident, was called in, but that official's powers being purely nominal he could do nothing, and the matter was given over to the chiefs, Dunn and Sibepu. Accordingly a force of about 1,500 of Sibepu's men, under Colenbrander, and 2,000 of Dunn's, led by the chief in person, met Sitimela and his followers, attacked and routed them with great loss, and burnt their military kraal. Sitimela himself was either slain or managed to get clean away, for he has not been heard of since, and peace was restored. The affair was seized upon with avidity by certain parties in Natal, stories of atrocities were trumped up, and capital made out of it by those interested in the King's return and others hostile to Dunn, who was accused of sanctioning the massacre of women and children, and encouraging his followers to commit acts of barbarity, and a small hullabaloo was raised. Of course some excesses are inevitable in war between savages, who in the flush of conquest are simply unrestrainable, but there is no proof that the chief was aware of any such until too late to prevent them, even if he was at all. On the other hand, I have been assured on good authority that his orders were the reverse of merciless. But a rising which might have assumed the proportions of a serious disturbance was effectually nipped in the bud by the promptitude and energy of John Dunn.

The chief has been severely handled by colonial writers and speakers on account of his attitude during the war—in fact denounced openly as a traitor to his former friends. Now this is not only unfair but ungrateful. Knowing every inch of the country, thoroughly conversant as one of

themselves with the people and their ways, Dunn
with his corps of Guides was able to be of the most
valuable service to our forces. Looked upon with
suspicion by the colonists as soon as he arrived in
Natal, and denounced as a Zulu spy ; his life in
danger as men's minds were more and more worked
up by the ever developing uncertainty and excitement attendant upon the war, what wonder that,
yielding to Lord Chelmsford's earnest solicitations,
he at length abandoned his attitude of neutrality
and took the field with us ? It was a mistake,
perhaps ; indeed I cannot help thinking that had
he held out to the end as strictly neutral, his position to-day would have been vastly stronger with
the Zulus themselves, and from a colonial point
unassailable. But, as he remarked rather bitterly
to me, his detractors never seemed to consider
what a difference it might have made to our arms
if he had thrown in his lot with Cetywayo and
brought European experience, combined with more
than Zulu shrewdness, to bear upon the enemy's
councils of war. That the Zulu force was badly
handled, not so much in open fight as in neglecting
to seize its multifold opportunities of harassing our
movements, is obviously patent ; what a difference,
then, in the results of the campaign might have
been the presence of a cool, resolute, far-seeing
European at its head.

John Dunn's history is briefly this. English by
birth, he arrived in Natal with his parents when
quite a boy, and early evinced a predilection for a
roving life. In 1856 civil war broke out in Zululand between Cetywayo, then heir to the throne,
and his brother Umbulazi, and Dunn, at that time
twenty-two years of age, was sent by the border
agent to assist the latter chieftain. The rival forces
met about four miles from the Tugela, close to
Mangéte, and a sanguinary battle took place, re-
sulting in the slaughter of Umbulazi, with a number
of his followers, and the total defeat of his army,
Dunn narrowly escaping by swimming the Tugela
and taking refuge in Natal.

In the course of hostilities, Cetywayo's party
had seized some cattle belonging to white traders
under the pretext that these had helped Umbulazi,
and this bid fair to lead to complications. Again
Dunn came to the fore, volunteering to proceed to
Cetywayo's residence and induce him to give up
the cattle. A risky experiment, deliberately to
place himself in the power of a savage ruler against
whom he had so recently fought. But he knew
his man; Cetywayo's ardour had had time to cool,
he saw that he had 'put his foot in it,' and was
casting about for a means of getting out of the
difficulty with a good grace. Dunn's arrival sup-
plied that means; the cattle were restored, and

Cetywayo, remembering the bravery displayed by
Dunn in battle, also admiring the cool daring of
the man who was not afraid to beard him in his
own country after having fought against him as
an enemy, made overtures of alliance. Dunn was
induced to transfer his fortunes to Zululand, where
he soon made his mark as a hunter and trader ; he
was created an *induna* over a section, and lived as
such under Cetywayo until the commencement of
hostilities in 1879.

The weather was too rainy during my stay for
much going about. On one occasion the chief took
me for a drive in his American ' spider,' and the
masterly way in which he steered that light but
thoroughly serviceable vehicle round the spurs and
along the steep grassy sides of the hills where there
wasn't a vestige of a track, rather astonished me.
' What would an English coachman do if told to
drive here ? ' said he. Certainly the feat looked a
formidable one, and yet we went swinging along
as if there had never been such a thing as a level
road. A younger brother of Cetywayo's, Gihlana
by name, put in an appearance at Ncandúku, but
there was nothing remarkable about him ; he has
a quiet, pleasing countenance, and, like the King,
is very dark coloured.

A strange and eventful life had been that of
my host, and, what with hunting stories and talking

over Zulu and other affairs, I found I had got
through three entertaining days by the time I took
the road again ; when, bidding farewell to the hospitable chief, I started across country under the
pilotage of a guide he had provided for me, to
rejoin the waggon at Etshowe.

CHAPTER XIII

Wild country—Sigcwelegcwele—A crack colonel of a crack regiment
—Etshowe again—A dissertation on phenomena—Inkwenkwe hill
—Vumandaba—A chief 'at Home'—'Hard wood'—A 'lively'
domicile—Novel weapons—'Bring us back the King!'

LEAVING Ncandúku behind, we struck into a narrow
bridle path which wound in and out around the tops
of the hills, the forest-clad Umgoye range on the
right, while to the left a rolling and sparsely wooded
tract of country stretched far away past the Gingindhlovu field to the Tugela. The day was cloudy
and cool, and my pony stepped out briskly; my
guide, a tall, thin old Zulu, trotting cheerily along
in front. Here and there we came to a multitude
of diverging tracks, whereupon the old fellow
would suddenly go down on all fours, minutely
examine the ground for a moment, and springing
up, point to one of the paths with his kerrie, ex-
claiming 'Lo!' (that), suiting the action to the
word by striding along it at a great pace. I was
fortunate to have him, for there were so many
tracks shooting off in all sorts of directions, that I

should have been sadly at sea if alone. Nor would
a knowledge of bearings help much, for the way is
so winding and circuitous, by reason of hills and
broken ground, that frequently you seem to be
heading right away from your destination instead
of towards it, and what is apparently the shortest
and most direct way leads you after a little while—
nowhere.

Thoroughly savage and forbidding in aspect
was the region through which lay my route that
morning, and yet essentially picturesque. On every
side deep ravines, a line of black vegetation
marking the course of a stream dashing through
their depths, while perched on a hilltop here and
there, might be seen a large kraal, its palisade of
thornbush, circular and symmetrical, forming a
dark crown upon the round green summit ; and as
we threaded the bridle path on the side of a well-
nigh perpendicular slope, literally poised over the
ravine hundreds of feet below, in our ears the
deafening rustle of the grassy sea swaying and
tossing in the breeze, the effect was certainly
wild.

Eight or ten miles of travelling brought us to
a couple of well-to-do-looking kraals, one being
that of Gihlana, before mentioned, the other that
of Sigcwelegcwele, the *induna* of the Ngobamakosi
regiment, which is the crack corps of the army.

I was anxious to visit this magnate, but had a long
way to go that day and the weather was very
unsettled; however, while debating in my mind
whether to go into the kraal or not, I saw a tall
Zulu advancing towards us from the drift of the
stream. From the deferential manner in which
my guide addressed him, I suspected that this must
be none other than the owner of the euphonious
name himself, and so it turned out. He is a fine-
looking man, in the prime of life, tall and broad-
shouldered, and carried his shaven head as erect
as if it ought to wear a crown instead of a shiny
ring of mimosa gum—a good specimen of a savage
warrior ; and I thought that if the Ngobamakosi
could show many men like its chief, small wonder
at it being the crack corps. We exchanged the
'time of day,' but not much more in the way of
indaba, and I held on my course. The Umlalasi at
that point boasts a remarkably bad drift, wherein,
my horse slipping, I came a nasty cropper, for-
tunately with no more result than a semi-ducking
and a bruised elbow. The old guide was active in
his commiseration, wrenching up huge handfuls of
grass wherewith he sought to dry my soaked
'continuations,' much in the way that one would
rub down a horse when grooming him. He
looked upon me as a special consignment from the
chief, and as such to be carefully handled until I

should be delivered over at Etshowe in safety. As we progressed I began to suspect that my pilot was by no means so sure of the road as he professed to be, and some curious turnings and awkward crossings which he ran me into, further strengthened the idea. However, we got over the worst and most hilly part of the way without further accident, and made a halt near the kraal of Sintwangu, the king's messenger, whom I had seen at the Inyoni. I sent the old fellow across to try and get some mealies or *tywala*, but he came back saying that Sintwangu was away, and the people at the kraal had told him that food was scarce in the land and they had none to spare ; so there was nothing for it but to saddle up again and push on. Notwithstanding this philosophical reflection I began to feel very hungry and rather tired, which combination of discomfort, taken in conjunction with my casualty in the drift, had thrown me—shall I confess it ?— into an exceedingly bad humour, culminating in the certainty that my guide was steering at random, in fact didn't know much about the way—a conviction I more than once endeavoured to force upon him, but the old fellow was very good-natured over it all—only laughed and shook his head, pointing to the track more emphatically than ever. I thought there was no end to the tortuosity of the bush paths—for we had got into wooded country again

—now slipping and tumbling in the rocky bed of a watercourse, now ducking my head to avoid having my eyes scratched out by the long sharp thorns of a sweeping mimosa bough, and was not at all sorry when, late in the afternoon, after a final climb, we found ourselves at Etshowe, and there, about a mile off on the flat, stood the white tent of the waggon.

My guide was well looked after, and started off home again next morning in a most contented frame of mind, brought about by the acquisition of sundry articles of luxury and use precious in native eyes.

And now I had come through the lower part of the country from end to end. Entering at Rorke's Drift, and taking the battlefields and places of interest in their order, I had thoroughly 'done' Isandhlwana and the Fugitives' Drift, Sirayo's stronghold, and the scene of the Prince Imperial's death in the Ityotyozi valley. I had inspected the fort at Etshowe, and the Inyezane battlefield, had made my way down to the residence of John Dunn near the Tugela mouth, and then round by the Gingindhlovu, Fort Crealock, and the Umgoye back to Etshowe. I had seen the different phases of country, wooded and open, and had had experience of all weathers. I had visited and been visited by several of the chiefs and principal personages, and had talked with all classes of the people. So now I began the return march. As far as Kwa-magwaza the way was the same ; from there I would branch off, and passing Ulundi make my way to the wild mountainous regions in the north.

Starting at daybreak from Etshowe, I intended to cross the Umhlatusi bush and get over the worst part of the opposite ascent before night, but the weather in front looked anything but promising. From the brow of the ridge heavy showers could be seen travelling along the opposite heights, com-pletely hiding them every now and then in a thick misty veil. Curious effects are frequent in these parts. I have watched a shower moving in a compact solid-looking pillar, and standing within a hundred yards of it as it swept by, felt no more of its effects than a slight drizzle, as one might feel the spray of a waterfall. I have stood for a couple of hours watching a violent thunderstorm sweep over a large tract, and within a mile of its inky curtain and vivid flashes, the clear azure of the sky imme-diately overhead was not obscured by a single fragment of a cloud. A beautiful effect was that produced by the change of position of a rainbow, one end of the bow remaining stationary, while the other described almost a semicircle on the plain, moving swiftly round like the beam of a revolving light in a fog. And the night side is rich in phenomena ; meteors of wondrous beauty are not infrequent, while shooting stars are so common that one hardly notices them.

Although the weather was dull and ominous, by afternoon the clouds had all cleared off, the sun poured his rays into the valley, keeping up its reputation for intense heat, which, by the way, is the usual characteristic of these deep bushy valleys. At nightfall I halted beneath the Inkwenkwe hill, whose round back loomed against the clear starry heavens. A flame from the dying camp fire every now and then cast a flickering glow upon the white tent, sinking again into its dull red embers ; the drowsy talk of the ' boys ' lying rolled in their blankets under the waggon ceased ; and the distant cry of bird or beast, borne up from the valley beneath, was the only sound which broke the stillness.

Between the Inkwenkwe and Kwamagwaza lives one of Cetywayo's military chiefs, by name Vumandaba, whom I had marked down for a visit; so under the guidance of a small boy who had wandered to the waggon to see what he could pick up, Andries and I started upon that mission. A winding bridle path, steep and slippery, brought us to the chief's residence, which lies in a deep valley—so deep and narrow as rigidly to exclude anything in the shape of a current of air. A

stifling hole; although but a short distance from
the road, one might pass it again and again without even suspecting the existence of habitation, so
uninviting and unlikely a place is it. The kraal is
not an imposing one by any means, and when we
arrived everything human seemed to be carefully
keeping out of the baking heat. A few draggle-
tailed cocks and hens were pecking about, and I
was rather astonished to see slinking among the
huts a common domestic cat, though a demoralised
and attenuated-looking specimen of the ' familiar '
of the kitchen hearth.

Dismounting in front of the principal tenement
amid vociferous yapping from the usual contingent
of curs, I was told that Vumandaba would be glad
to see me, so, crawling through the aperture, stood
up in the hut. Coming suddenly into the gloomy
interior from the full glare of a midday sun, at
first I could see no one, but soon made out several
dark forms squatting in a semicircle, upright and
motionless, eyeing me in suspicious and inquiring
silence. The chief was sitting a little apart from
the others, and having narrowly scrutinised me for
a few moments, he broke the silence with the usual
greeting, ' Saku bona! ' to which I responded by
shaking hands, and sat down opposite him. The
Zulu has a mode of shaking hands peculiar to

himself; it is not like the English way, but a good honest grip for all that. His fingers and thumb are kept quite rigid, but he lays hold of your hand and shakes it with a will; very different to the dab of a flabby paw with which the Boer favours you, leaving a sensation on your palm, of contact with a fish or a raw leg of mutton. Vumandaba is a tall, thin old man, with grizzled hair and beard, a rugged countenance, and at first a not very prepossessing appearance; he is a good specimen of the high class Zulu, dignified in manner and speech, and free from Dabulamanzi's besetting sin—begging. He was in great favour with Cetywayo, who created him principal *induna* over the Kandampemvu regiment, and also appointed him 'cupbearer,' his duties being to attend upon the King and to taste the food and drink before it was allowed to pass the royal palate.

I said that Vumandaba's appearance was not a prepossessing one; yet, when the first instincts of native reserve had worn off, I found him a very genial and pleasant old fellow. Not the least pleasing feature about him were his feelings of attachment and loyalty towards his late master. He was full of Cetywayo, nearly his first question being about the King and his welfare. 'Why hadn't we brought him back? All the people wanted

him. When Lukuni[1] (Sir Evelyn Wood) came to
Inhlazatye several moons ago they thought he was
bringing back Cetywayo, but instead he told them
that the King would not be restored. They were
disappointed; they all wanted the King again.
Why had Lukuni come all the way from England
to tell them that? *I* must get the King brought
back to them; they wanted to see him. When I
returned home I must be sure and tell the Government to send back Cetywayo.'

I hastened to explain that my mission in Zululand was quite unofficial, and that, being only a
private person, I had no more influence for or
against the desired restoration than the most
insignificant inhabitant of their kraal. But it
was no use; they only half believed me, for they
couldn't understand anyone taking the trouble to
visit them and their country purely for the fun of
the thing. 'Hadn't I *anything* to do with Lukuni
or with Government?' 'Nothing whatever,' I
reiterated. I told the old chief, however, that I
could do this much for him—record his wishes for
the benefit of the public. Whereat he seemed
pleased.

There was one exceedingly unpleasant side to

[1] 'Lukuni' means literally 'hard wood,' and the sobriquet by
which the gallant General is known throughout Zululand is not only
a play upon his name, but a tribute to his reputation as a soldier in
native es:imation.

my visit. Happening to glance upwards I noticed that the whole roof of the hut was alive with a kind of trembling shimmer, reminding one of the electric advertisements over shop doors. On closer investigation I discovered that the roof was alive with cockroaches, whose shiny backs were responsible for the glistening I had seen. They literally swarmed, and though with some alacrity I left a space between myself and the side of the hut against which I had been leaning, yet every now and then one of the cheerful insects would playfully promenade along my ear, or two or three would organise a steeplechase on the brim of my wide-awake. This was nasty, to say the least of it, but when they took to dropping into the pots of *tywala* which had been brought in for our delectation, it was nastier. The old chief didn't seem to care though ; with the greatest *sangfroid* he would insert his grass spoon, ladle out the offending insect, and proceed to take a big drink on the spot, just to show there was no ill feeling ; while I—well, the day was piping hot, and one can't afford to be fastidious in the wilds—found it in my conscience to follow his example. All the native huts, by the way, are more or less overrun with cockroaches, though in some of comparatively recent construction there are hardly any ; Vumandaba's abode, however, judging by the smoke-blackened rafters and the superabundance of these crawling pests, must have been a venerable tenement indeed.

The Kandampemvu regiment was in the thick of the battle at Isandhlwana, and foremost in carrying the camp, though it suffered severely in the earlier stage of the conflict from the fire of the outlying companies; and now its chief told me how stubbornly some of our soldiers had fought to the last, many of them using their pocket-knives when their bayonets were wrenched from them. Some even astonished their savage enemies by a well-directed ' one, two ' straight from the shoulder, flooring the too exultant warriors like nine-pins. The Zulus could not understand how men could use their hands as knob kerries, for the native is quite a stranger to the art of fisticuffs. ' A few of the soldiers,' said the chief, ' shot a great deal with " little guns " (revolvers), but they didn't shoot well. For every man they killed, they fired a great many shots without hitting anybody.'

One thing that sent Vumandaba up in my estimation was that he did not begin by asking for anything and everything. But although he did not beg, he was greatly delighted with the gift of a large knife and a few other things I had brought, gripping my hand with fervent expressions of thanks, which were duly echoed by the other men in the hut; for if you give anything to a chief, his followers always shout out their thanks as vigorously as though the donation were to each and all of themselves. He made me a present of a likely-looking knob-kerrie ' to remember him by,' which I have still—a most effective companion for a dark road in a ruffianly neighbourhood. On hearing I would pass Inhlazatye, he was very anxious that I should see Mnyamane and the King's son Dinizulu, and as I was getting up to go, the old chief laid his hand on my arm in his eagerness. ' Bring us back Cetywayo,' he said ; ' we want to see our King again. Bring him back ! ' I declare I felt quite small for the moment, call it foolish sentimentality who will. Many a time since have I seemed to see the old man's rugged, earnest face, and to hear his emphatic tones—the loyal old warrior—pleading for his fallen and exiled King.

CHAPTER XIV

Cetywayo and the missionaries—Entonjaneni—Valley of the White Umfolosi—A cool spot and a picture—Mahlabatini—'Then and now'—Battle of Ulundi.

HITHERTO I had been particularly fortunate, having got along without breakdown or accident of any sort, either to waggon or oxen, servants or self, and now was back at Kwamagwaza. There I met Dr. Oftebro, a Norwegian medical missionary, who had been some time settled in the country and was then living in the Mahlabatini basin, a few miles from Ulundi. This gentleman—a relation, by the way, of the missionary at Etshowe—was of opinion that the war could not have been averted. The Zulus, he said, especially the younger men, were so inflated with martial ardour, so completely carried away by a sense of their own vast superiority over any force that could be brought against them, that there was absolutely no holding them ; and they bragged openly and incessantly of what they could and would do when the word was given for them to march upon Natal. In fact,

a white man's life was not safe in Zululand at the
time. The doctor had no very high opinion of
Cetywayo, whom he described as crafty and un-
reliable, infinitely inferior in character and probity
to his father Mpande,[1] whose word could always
be depended upon.

By the way, I found that Cetywayo did not
stand well with the missionaries generally, which one
can readily understand ; for, apart from a certain
professional prejudice against a man who deliberately and absolutely rejected their teachings, all
the traditions, interests, and predilections of a
savage ruler, or, indeed, of a civilised one, would
naturally be in antagonism to the setting up of an
imperium in imperio among his subjects. That the
establishment of mission stations was regarded
distrustfully by Cetywayo on this account there
can be no doubt ; and if ' good ' and well-meaning
people would but think, they would see that a
heathen king was not necessarily a monster because
he opposed the ' spread of the Gospel,' and
would, perhaps, write and talk a little less wild
nonsense on the subject. Even if the would-be
evangelisers are earnest, single-minded men, desirous
only of making converts from heathenism—as I am
willing to believe the missionaries in Zululand are—
the fact still remains that the whole of their

[1] Commonly known as Pánda.

teaching is contrary to the most rooted convictions and time-honoured customs of the nation, upon whom, after all, they are virtually forced *nolens volens*. I say forced, because it is idle to suppose that, prior to the war more than now, any Zulu potentate would have *dared* actually to abolish missions, however desirous he might be of doing so. It is one thing for the missionary to take his life in his hand and go among savages, simply relying on his message and example for success; it is another thing for him to go into Zululand with the full *moral* support of the British Government at his back. I have no hostility towards missionaries as such—quite the contrary. But I do think we should look at the question from both sides ; remembering, too, that in his heathen state the Zulu would not compare badly for morality and honesty with the average Briton, man for man, and that Christianity is not always exhibited to him in a specially immaculate or attractive guise. And it is a fact that no missionary's life was ever taken or even threatened in Zululand previous to the war or since, though they may now and then have undergone petty annoyances from this or that individual chief.

A midday halt some twelve miles from Kwa-magwaza, a night trek, a long bumping down the steep Entonjaneni hill, and we are among the 'thorns' in the valley of the White Umfolosi. Stifling hot is it here, even so early as 7 A.M., and as we move along towards the river not a sign of humanity do we see. No picturesque kraals dotting the hill sides; we meet no Zulus striding along the road flinging their cheery greeting at us as they pass; all is deserted even as though the land were 'dead,' as the expressive native idiom for war-time has it. Here and there a huge bird of prey springs away from the topmost branches of a euphorbia, and, spreading his broad wings, soars lazily off to flop down upon a bough some two hundred yards further and inspect the intruders; or a buck starts up suddenly amid the long grass, and before I can get a shot at him, bounds off through the thick bush which covers the valley on either hand. Passing the old *laager* where the column was lying four days before the battle, while messages were exchanged between the King and Lord Chelmsford, we come to the drift, which, though wide, is shallow and good. We cross, and outspan on the bank under the shade of the mimosas. It is a lovely spot. In front the broad Umfolosi flows on over its sands, between green banks fringed with overhanging trees and dense reed patches, then, making a sudden bend below the drift, it washes the base of a long wall of red *krantz* whose cre-viced face is festooned with mosses and trailing ferns. The air is warm but not sultry, and vibrates ever and anon with the strident screech of a tree cricket, while the call and whistle of many a bird sounds from the brake. ·Presently some Zulus descend to the river on the other side, and begin to cross; the effect of their dark bodies against the water, their coloured shields and gleaming assegais, and the wild surrounding, with the background of bush and blue sky, makes a perfect picture. Then as the sun gets low, we inspan and trek on quietly, to halt upon the scene of the great decisive battle which was to break the Zulu power.

From the Umfolosi drift, open and undulating ground with patches of bush here and there. We cross a small watercourse or two, and about an hour's travelling brings us to a grassy level, commanding a view of the entire plain, from the river behind to the ranges of hills which close it in like a basin. Here on the right, about one hundred yards from the road, is the site of the Nodwengu kraal; about a mile on the other side of it is a huge circle in the grass, several hundred yards in diameter. A curious circle, apparently a belt of herbage of different growth, for it is darker than the green slope on which it lies. That circle is all that remains of the Ulundi kraal—the former residence of the Zulu King. About a mile beyond this again, and at nearly even distances from each other, may

be seen two more large circles, marking the site of
the military kraals, Qikazi and Umlambongwenya,
the first being on the left and nearest the road.
The remaining two, Undakaombi and Bulawayo,
situate on the left of the road and not visible from
it, go to make up the six kraals constituting the
capital of Zululand. Whether by accident or
design they are placed in threes, forming two
triangles.

Travelling through the country I think one
hardly realises to the full the thoroughness of its
conquest. Kraals and mealie fields all over the
place ; cattle grazing quietly and securely ; Zulus
passing to and fro, always cheerful and apparently
contented, and to hear them talk, moreover, does
not convey the idea of a conquered people. But
standing as I did that sunny afternoon contemplat-
ing the large silent circles on the Mahlabatini
plain, formerly astir with busy life—then it is that
the sense of change forces itself upon one.

Let us suppose an evening such as this. There
stand the huge kraals with their clustering rings
of dome-shaped huts, among which, here and there,
dark forms may be seen moving, while yonder a
number of women are coming from the stream,
calabash on head, in single file, stepping to the
time of a monotonous but not unmelodious chant.
The sun dips to the western hills ; sleek cattle are

wending along the green plain, conspicuous among
them the snowy whiteness of the royal herd ; the
barking of dogs and the shout and whistle of drivers
mingling with the deep-toned low of driven cattle.
For a short time all is bustle and animation ; then
the red fires twinkle out here and there in the
fast gathering darkness ; a hush falls ; but those
silent and fantastic dwellings are teeming with
human life—the pulsating heart of a warrior
nation.

But to-day how different is all this. Yon
silent circles remain, sole relics of the savage
capital burnt and razed to the ground. Our shot
and shell has well and effectually done its work.
Skulls and bones bleaching by hundreds in the
grassy bottoms, instead of the fierce and dauntless
savages who formerly peopled this place and
marched in serried battalions up to the very mouth
of the cannon, to be mown down like grass, but to
fall as valiant warriors, shouting their battle cry—
as true patriots defending their homes. No one
can say that these were foemen unworthy of our
steel, and now that resentment has had time to
cool, no one will grudge them due praise for a long
and stubborn defence of their country. But the
blood of thousands of their bravest has been
poured out like water, their King a captive and an
exile—their former capital a scene of silence and

desolation. Truly one feels that the greatness of a nation lies buried here.

The following is so graphic an account of the battle of Ulundi that I cannot refrain from quoting it in full. It appeared in the ' Port Elizabeth Telegraph,' August 12, 1879.

BATTLE OF ULUNDI.
(*By an Eye-witness.*)

' Some weeks have elapsed since I wrote to you last, and during the interval some stirring events have come to pass. I must make a skip and come down to July 2. On that day the two brigades of the second division, having on the day previous descended from the heights to the west of Ulundi, began the march which brought them, in the afternoon, to the banks of the White Umvolosi. In the early morning, long before the sun was up, Col. Buller, that man of muscle and nerve, had started with his irregular but serviceable cavalry to take up a position on the west bank of the river, and hold it until joined by the troops. At six o'clock the column followed, the 90th leading. I left at the time, and an hour's ride brought me to the cavalry. The mounted infantry, under Capt. Brown, were away on a distant ridge to the left, the Basutos, under Captain Cochrane, were ahead, Raaff's Rangers were on the right, and D'Arcy's

F.L.H., with Baker's Horse, were in the centre.
Everything was quiet when I arrived, although
a few minutes before the men had distinctly heard
the war song of a Zulu regiment in motion.
Hearing from Capt. Blaine that this regiment could
be seen from the position held in front by the
Basutos, I went forward and joined these gallant
auxiliaries. I found them all seated upon a small
kopje, and, together with their officers, looking
intently at the kraal of Nodwengu, distant from
there about four miles. They had been watching
the regiment whose chanting had been heard by
the volunteers behind. This regiment or regiments
numbered about 8,000, and came from a military
kraal about five miles to the north-west of Nodwengu, and on the left of the Basutos. The Zulus
marched in companies, chanting their terrible war
song as they went, and very soon reached Nodwengu, into which they filed in splendid order.
From the kopje I had a good view of Undine,
which I take to mean a collection of the King's
kraals. Below us, 800 yards off, flowed the winding Umvolosi, its western bank covered with a
thick growth of mimosa trees and aloes; just before
us, and a mile on the other side of the river, was
Bulawayo, one of the military kraals ; to the right
of that, and 700 yards distant, was the mighty
circle of Nodwengu, with its ring of huts, five

deep; to the east of the latter was another large military kraal; another one again on the right of this, and between these two last, but nearer down, was Ulundi, with the southern curve of the circle alone showing on the top of a rise. It was not long before I saw the regiment leave Nodwengu and march for a kraal above it. In half-an-hour I saw four regiments on the march from various points to a kraal above Ulundi. In this they formed up, and a formidable mass they appeared to be; almost filling up all the available space in the huge circle. Ulundi, you must remember, is 500 yards in diameter, and the other kraals are almost as large. At 12 o'clock the formation broke up, and the warriors poured out in three broad and long black columns. They had been doctored, and were ready to accept battle. However, no engagement was to be fought that day. General Chelmsford would not cross the river, although the ground on the other bank offered by far the best site for a camp; and the two laagers were formed up among the thorn trees at a distance of some 700 yards from the river drift.'

After describing at considerable length the events of July 3, the narrator goes on :

'Next morning, ere yet the sun had risen, the troops silently assembled. Buller's Irregulars crossed the river and took up a position at the Bula-

wayo kraal. At 6 o'clock the infantry advanced,
Wood's division leading. The Lancers brought
up the rear. The morning was biting, and a damp
mist hung over the river, but the troops walked
through the broad river as if they were tramping
along over a macadamised road. The march was
continued to the Bulawayo kraal, where the troops
were formed up in square, while the cavalry
advanced again as far as Nodwengu. General
Wood then rode forward and selected a spot to the
north-east of Nodwengu, and about 600 yards from
the nearest curve of the huts. This site was on
a ridge, and commanded a front on every side of
500 yards. While the troops were advancing to
take up a position here, the irregular cavalry
again moved onward. At this time the mist was
lifting, and the enemy could be seen on our right
and left advancing in loose and open order. I
went up to Baker's Horse, who were ordered to
draw on the enemy from the north. Very soon I
saw the loose masses on the north form up in
companies, which soon covered a frontage of a
mile, with the right wing resting on a ridge above
the drift, and the left wing in the valley on the
north side. As Baker's Horse advanced another
body of the enemy emerged from the hills still
further north, formed into line, and effected a
junction with the other line. There was then a

horse-shoe formation on the north, with the right
on one ridge and the left on another, and covering
a distance of some three miles. This long black
line swept steadily forward upon us, and, as I
saw them come on, I thought the battle that day
would be a long and a terrible one. Baker's Horse
advanced towards the left wing of this formation,
and as they neared the regiment on the left the
latter broke up, and the Zulus scattered in skirmishing order. Lieut. Parmenter then advanced
with about twenty men, and poured a volley
into the enemy at a distance of about 200 yards.
The cavalry then slowly retired. They had done
what was required. This had drawn on the enemy
in fine style, and as we galloped back to the square
the bullets were whizzing about us. Just before
Lieut. Parmenter made his daring advance I looked
around. Not a shot had been fired. The mist
was slowly lifting from the hills, but still hung
above the river. The sun was flaming blood red
above the eastern hills. All was quiet ; an awful
stillness brooded over the valley, broken only by
the melodious singing of birds, a strange prelude
to thunder of cannon and rattle of musketry.
Nature seemed waiting for the terrible drama to
be so soon played out on that silent plain. Silent
and motionless for that breathless instant were
those who were to play at that drama. Below us

was the solid square of British soldiers, a small red square, the centre of a vast black line formed by 15,000 savage warriors, who were here bearded in their stronghold.   Between the centre and the black line were bodies of cavalry scattered, each troop standing in line with front to the enemy.   It seems to us that the black line has but to tighten and then, with a rush and a bound as it springs into action, overwhelm that small body of British soldiers.   But there are terrors concealed in that solid square that will shake the fiercest hearts and boldest spirits among the Zulu thousands.   See that cloud of white smoke that suddenly sweeps from a corner of the square !   Hark to that thunderous report ; hear the rushing of the shell overhead !   The battle has commenced ; the circle is drawing in ; the cavalry are retreating ; the first gun has been fired ; the shell breaks above the heads of a regiment of hot young men advancing at a run from the north, and as it breaks those beneath scatter and rush back.   If Cetywayo, watching the battle from afar, sees that he must quake.   When men waver in the first rush there is little hope for them.   But still the circle narrows, and now the cavalry are all within the four walls of living men.   Then the roar of battle begins indeed.   There is one continuous rattle of musketry all round the square, the thunder of guns,

the growling of the Gatlings, and the constant
whizzing of the bullets overhead. The 94th and
21st form the rear ; the 58th and 13th face Nodwengu on the right ; the 80th are in front, and the
90th on the left. There are two guns at every
corner, and two guns in the centre of each side.
Young regiments are attacking the rear and left ;
married men on the right and front. The enemy
makes the fiercest assault on the rear. On come
the young men in the face of the leaden hail
poured upon them by the 94th and 21st. These
regiments are as cool as if on parade, and they fire
in sections, obeying the orders of their officers as
to sighting and firing. They keep up a continual
firing, but yet the young warriors advance until
they are within one hundred yards. Now there is
a cry for the Gatlings, and the order is passed
down the line of the 90th to the 80th. Now the
enemy are within one hundred yards of the glistening bayonets ; and now they waver and look back.
It is all over with them. A thundering cheer from
volunteers and soldiers rises above the roar of
guns. The enemy turns and flies. Now is the
time for the Lancers. They leap into their saddles,
and the 21st open a way for them, but the General
thinks it is too early for a charge. Besides, the
married regiments are making it warm for the
13th and 58th. A few more volleys are fired, and

then the Lancers are permitted to go. They file
out and form up outside the 94th ; their tall lances
and fluttering pennons look like a forest. Now
they are off, and are thundering after the dis-
heartened warriors. They sweep round from the
right of the 94th, and come out at the left of the
21st, and their track is marked by some 150 dead
and dying Zulus. And now the irregular cavalry
dash out. Baker's Horse rushes up to the point it
reached in the morning, and chases the very regiment it had drawn on. The Basutos gallop away
towards Ulundi, chasing one of Cetywayo's picked
regiments beyond the King's kraal and killing
some 50 warriors. And so with the other troops.
The battle has lasted but 40 minutes. We lost
16 killed and had about 40 wounded. Truly
the Zulus are bad shots, for a better target than
we presented they could not have wished for.
The enemy lost about 1,500, and 500 of these we
must put to the account of the cavalry, who, both
English and colonial, behaved splendidly. Half-
an-hour after Ulundi was in flames. It was a huge
kraal, with huts six deep, and in numbers sufficient
to shelter 10,000 men. I went into Cetywayo's
house (a three-roomed single-floored place, with
thatched roof, verandah, doors, and windows), but
there was nothing in it but some old rat traps
and three pieces of ivory, which fell to the lot

respectively of Commandant Baker, Lord Beresford (who was first in the kraal), and Capt. Cochrane, who fired the house. In an hour the six military kraals on the plain were in flames and belching forth dense volumes of smoke. That night the Zulus sang a different song from that which they had so menacingly wailed forth on the preceding night. The battle was decided by the artillery before the enemy came within range of the small arms. The shrapnel took the dash out of the attacking columns. The enemy's strategy was excellent, but its execution was bad. Cetywayo, as I have said, watched the battle from afar in company with Mnyamane and other chiefs. Dabulamanzi was present at the fight.'

CHAPTER XV

MY camp was pitched within thirty yards of
the site of the famous hollow square and about
four hundred from that of Nodwengu, and the
morning after arrival I started to explore the ruins
of Ulundi, under the guidance of an old Zulu who
had formerly been one of the head men of the
Undakaombi kraal. At the bottom of the slope I
dismounted to examine one or two of the skulls
lying about among the grass, some being remarkably large and well developed ones. I drew my
guide's attention to this, as he stood curiously
watching me. The old man smiled rather mourn-
fully and shook his head. 'Yes,' he said, 'we lost
some fine men—numbers of them. What could we
do against you English ? You stand still, and only
by turning something round[1] make the bodies of
our warriors fly to pieces ; legs here, arms there,
heads, everything. Whouw !—What can we do

[1] The Gatling.

against that?' We resumed our way, and having crossed the stream which threads in sedgy reaches along the grassy bottom, stood upon the ruins of Ulundi.

Some idea as to the dimensions of the kraal may be gleaned when I say that it takes full five minutes of tolerably quick walking to cross it. The floors of the huts still remain, with their fire-places in the centre, but are thickly overgrown with coarse herbage. At the upper end, near the principal gateway, was Cetywayo's residence, a square tenement with glazed windows and a door; the other huts for his wives and attendants being of the ordinary shape. I was keenly on the look-out for relics, but could find none; a few bits of broken glass, remnants of ancient gin bottles, lay about, and fragments of native pottery, which is made of clay baked in the sun and very brittle and crumbly. On the site of the King's huts I picked up some pieces of a clay bowl, a fragment of an iron three-legged pot, and a smooth round stone such as would be used for polishing floors—a duty it had probably often performed on that of the royal dwelling. Other relics more curious or valuable there were none.

We pass on to Nodwengu. Here everything wears a similar aspect, and the floors of the huts clustering thickly together are covered with the same rank overgrowth. Nodwengu is the next in size and importance to Ulundi, and like it, a royal residence, having been the abode of the last King, Mpande, Cetywayo's father. It is now the head-quarters of the Nodwengu and Kandampemvu regiments—Ulundi, as its name implies, being that of the Undi, the royal corps.

By the time we have fully explored the two homes of former royalty, the increasing force of a blazing midday sun renders it expedient to return to the shade of the waggon, where, as I lay in the heat of the afternoon, taking it easy in company with a long pipe, a passer by or two would sit down for a few minutes' chat, but people were not so numerous in these parts as I should have expected. One young Zulu, a light-hearted, talk-ative fellow, sat there descanting by the hour on things in general. He had been shot in the leg at Isandhlwana soon after the fight commenced, and had lain on the ground until two of his brothers carried him out of harm's way, so was not able to see the end. I put in a suggestion to the effect that it was better to be shot through the leg at the beginning of the fight than through the head at the end of it, which aspect of the case seemed vastly to tickle his imagination, for he went into a fit of laughter and agreed emphatically with the idea. I happening to mention that I was rather on the look-out for curiosities, my friend produced a beautiful little horn snuffbox, and wanted to know if that was the kind of thing. I replied that it was, whereupon he handed it over with a laugh, saying I must take it to show the people in England. He then asked if he should get me any more like it, and on receiving an answer in the affirmative he limped off down the road, returning in about half-an-hour with a lot of snuffboxes, bangles, spoons, and beadwork trifles, for which he said I must give him things in exchange, as they were not his own, and he couldn't make me a present of them as he did the first snuffbox. I took over the lot, to our mutual satisfaction. Poor fellow, he will carry a tangible reminder of that bullet until his dying day.

While on the subject, I was surprised at the fewness of wounded men I fell in with during my progress through the country. Whether, owing to rude surgery, numbers died whom the most ordinary skill could easily have saved, I cannot say, but considering that every man with whom I conversed had taken part in one or more of the battles, the fewness of those who had wounds to show *was* rather remarkable.

Presently some girls put in an appearance, with the object of bartering a mat to me in exchange for some beads. I looked at the mat—it was a

good specimen of native work, and would do well
to hang a Zulu trophy against, when my travels
had been relegated to events of the past—and
decided to have it. But the way in which the
artless young creatures haggled was amazing. I
hadn't the exact kind of beads they wanted, so
must give them about five times as many of
another kind; and that wasn't enough either; I
must throw in half-a-dozen other things besides,
because I was an 'inkos,' and they didn't see a
white 'inkos' every day, and so on. I let them
have their full fling, and then stated my terms.
More haggling, all talking at once, chattering and
laughing at the top of their voices; but I got my
mat, and at my own price.

Our bargain concluded, they seemed sorry there
was nothing else to wrangle over, if only for an
excuse to make a little more noise. Two of them
were daughters of the old man who had officiated
as guide in the morning; another argument adduced
in favour of an extra donation, by the way. Many
of the Zulu girls are good looking; tall and graceful, with an exceedingly bright and pleasing expression; and these two were no bad specimens of
their race, as they stood there, their lithe brown
figures adorned with various coloured beads
fantastically worked. They made such a row,
however, chattering and screaming with laughter,

that I was not sorry to see the last of them, as they went bounding away in the direction of the paternal kraal.

A glorious night succeeds the heat of the day ; one advantage of the South African climate is that however hot the day, the night is nearly sure to be at any rate bearably cool. This one is perfect ; the air still and balmy without a suspicion of chilliness, and not until after midnight can I make up my mind to turn in, so take a late stroll round the scene of the conflict. A grand moon in its third quarter hangs overhead ; shadowy and indistinct sleep the heights, bathed in a misty film, the sharp outline of many a peak toned down by the softening light ; a faint murmur of plashing water is just audible, where Umfolosi flows and ripples over her sandy bed ; and ever and anon, from far away along the bushy river bank, the howl of some prowling beast is borne upon the night. I wander on ; at every step skulls, gleaming white amid the grass, grin to the moon with upturned face and eyeless sockets. Yonder, shadowed forth in dark contrast on the moonlit plain, lie the ruins of Ulundi and Nodwengu, dim and mysterious, like mystic tracings from the wand of some grim wizard of the wilderness. A night bird skims across the waste, its plaintive cry floating above the weird circles like a strange lament over the downfall of those who erewhile peopled these solitudes, and a slight breeze shudders through the long grass like the whisperings of unearthly voices.

I return to camp, the white tent of the waggon glistens like silver in the moonbeams, and a few dull red embers in the dying fire glow amid the ashes. Every living thing, biped and quadruped, is buried in slumber, an example I haste to follow.

CHAPTER XVI

IT is early morning as we move away from our
halting place and take the road for Inhlazatye,
which runs right past the kraal of Mfanawendhlela,
the chief of the Ulundi district, who tumbles out,
swathed in a green blanket, to prefer a modest
request for a bottle of gin. He is, however, doomed
to disappointment.

We climb the ridge, and the road winds along
the heights above the Mahlabatini plain ; there lie
the circles of the ruined kraals, the silver thread of
the river is now and again visible, and beyond, the
stone wall of the old laager ; while rising from the
wide valley, the Entonjaneni range cleaves the sky-
line. Turning from this to the north-eastward a
view of the dark forests beyond the Black Umfolosi opens out. A few hours' travelling, and we
reach a group of large kraals standing surrounded

by their mealie patches, and bearing every indica-
tion of well-to-do-ness.   So unusual a sight as a
tent waggon and its team, and a Briton riding in
front of the same, was enough to cause quite a
commotion in the minds of the inhabitants, and
in less than no time half a dozen big Zulus came
running up, anxious to know who I was and all
about me ; as usual, taking me for a trader.   They
pointed out a good place to outspan, and I told
them to come down presently and have a talk ; a
proposal they were ready enough to endorse, for, as
I said before, the Zulu is an inveterate gossip, and
given a good listener, will indulge his propensity
for *indaba* to any extent.   Over and above which,
an idea is floating through his mind that there are
pickings to be got at the white man's waggon, and
that on leaving the said structure he is extremely
likely to have acquired sundry trifles of more or
less value to himself.

These were exceedingly civil fellows.   We had
not outspanned many minutes before a lot of
amasi[1] was brought to us, sent by the head of
the kraal, who with two or three more came to see
what was going on.   Others ' dropped in,' and
presently there were ten or a dozen stalwart bar-

---

[1] Curdled milk, which forms the staple article of Zulu diet.   It is
eaten with mealies or ' amabele,' worked into a kind of paste.   No
adult Zulu will touch fresh milk, which is looked upon as food only
fit for children.

barians squatting round, talking and laughing at a great rate. I think there can hardly exist a more thoroughly good-humoured race than these people; they never seem out of spirits, always cheerful and lively, ready at a jest too. And can't they laugh? Anything in the shape of a joke will elicit roars of merriment, spontaneous, hearty, and unfeigned. I have seen a group of Zulus roll on the ground and laugh till the tears ran down their cheeks, at the antics and repartee of a native Joe Miller. My visitors on the present occasion formed no exception to the rule. They talked and sang, and went through various manœuvres for my entertainment, showing me how they made the charges which proved so fatal to our troops. They would rush forward about fifty yards, and imitating the sound of a volley, drop flat amid the grass; then when the firing was supposed to have slackened, up they sprung, and assegai and shield in hand charged like lightning upon the imaginary foe, shouting ' Usútu.' It certainly gave one a very fair idea of their mode of procedure in actual warfare.

I wanted to reach Inhlazatye that day—its forest-clad sides were visible, rising up far in front—so as soon as the heat began to abate, prepared for a start. When we had inspanned, the head man made a speech, consisting, as usual under the cir-

cumstances, of expressions of good will, after which
the Zulus stood up, and with hand uplifted sang
out, ' Inkos ! Hambane gahlé ! ' [1] their deep voices
making quite an imposing chorus. We parted the
best of friends, and saddling up I mounted and took
the road, leaving the waggon to follow.

A long, deep, desolate valley stretching ahead
for miles—a spectacle to rejoice the eyes of a lover
of the wild open scenery of Dartmoor and the like.
The hill sides treeless and brown, nothing to relieve
the wild monotony of the bare grassy slopes ; a
clear stream dashing over rocks and boulders ; the
jagged outlines of the mountain ridges, prominent
above which rise the terraced slopes of the turret-
headed Zihlalu ; and the utter sense of solitude,
would, I repeat, form a paradise to the moorland
rambler. But to me there always seems something
dismal about this kind of thing. The stillness, the
absence of animal life, all has a sombre and depressing influence, as of a place one would be glad to
get out of. Every now and then the track would
descend abruptly into a watercourse overhung with
precipitous rocks and aloes, just the place for an
ambuscade. A steady climb up a long steep bit of
road, and I am riding over wide elevated table-
lands ; behind, the towering head of Zihlalu, which
from this point bears a striking resemblance to the

----

[1] 'Chief! go in peace !'

lion-shaped Isandhlwana, diminishes against the evening sky, the wooded sides of Inhlazatye draw nearer and nearer, and presently a light twinkles from a group of huts at the base of the mountain. It is the Residency.

Here a disappointment awaited, for the British Resident, Mr. Osborn, whom I was anxious to see, had left for Maritzburg only that morning ; but I met with a very kind welcome from his clerk, Mr. Boast, who was in charge during the absence of his chief. The Residency, which is structurally of a significantly temporary nature, consisting in fact of a few large Zulu huts, occupies a pleasant site on the eastern slope of Inhlazatye, commanding a wide sweep of hill and valley in front, while im-mediately behind, the great mountain rears its forest-clad sides and precipitous walls. Mr. Osborn and his clerk were the only Europeans on the place, a few native policemen and an interpreter or two constituting the staff, under which circum-stances it may readily be imagined that the sole influence exercisable by Her Majesty's British Resident in Zululand must be of the order known as moral suasion. It may likewise be supposed that, situated in the midst of a number of turbulent and discontented chiefs and rival factions in a chronic state of almost open warfare, among whom the peace must be kept somehow, two Europeans,

backed by a few native constables, are in a somewhat precarious and difficult position. Such was
the state of Zululand and the position of its
Resident at the time of my progress through the
country.

From the summit of Inhlazatye, a wide plateau
some 6,000 feet above the sea level, there is a
grand view, the whole country lying mapped out
beneath. It is one of the highest points in Zululand, and with Ibabanango constitutes quite a land-
mark for the greater part of the western side—
either of which when visible would suffice to in-
dicate his bearings to anyone not wholly deficient
in bump of locality. Capital company was my
host, and as we sat of an evening—shall I confess
it ?—till late, over our pipes, he would entertain me
by the hour with anecdotes of Diamond Fields and
border interest. An isolated monotonous sort of
life must this Residency position be, but my friend
Mr. Boast seemed to take to it kindly. There
were horses to ride and plenty of bucks to be shot
in the mountains, whose grassy slopes also abounded
in partridges and quail ; it cost not much in the
way of living, and life could be taken in free and
easy fashion.

Very cheerless was the prospect as, after a stay
of three days at Inhlazatye, I turned out of one of
the huts at early dawn and climbed shiveringly

into the saddle, having started the waggon the previous day. The air was chilly, heavy masses of grey mist were driving along the face of the cliff, a general feeling of dampness and a lowering sky seemed to portend rain, and amid so auspicious an opening to another day, I turned my back on the Residency and struck into the road which skirts the northern side of the mountain. On the one hand a mighty cliff, whose dark wall frowned overhead, on the other extensive fields of mealies and *amabele*, with kraals in the distance; but being in about as exalted a state of spirits as the gloomy surroundings and the weather would be likely to produce, I hardly looked to the right or to the left as my pony stepped along at a brisk easy walk, till, going down into a drift to cross a dry watercourse, my cogitations were suddenly interrupted by a deep threatening sound, and above the long grass on the opposite bank appeared a formidable-looking head, surmounted by a pair of sharp gleaming horns with a most suggestive upward curve, the whole being the property of a very fine and very savage-looking Zulu bull, who stood there about ten yards in front, rolling the whites of his eyes, and pawing the ground with all the power and more than half the will to oppose my progress; for that the deep growling sound which he emitted was the bovine equivalent for

' no thoroughfare,' neither I nor my steed entertained the slightest doubt. Now I was not at all
in the humour to make a long détour just for the
sake of affording a little fun to my opponent, and
yet there the brute stood, lashing his chocolate-
coloured hide, ploughing up the earth with his
hoofs, and throwing his horns about in a manner
that meant volumes.   What was to be done ?—my
most formidable weapon of offence or defence being
two thirds of a light riding switch.   However,
' needs must, &c.;' so turning a little out of the
track I passed about a dozen yards from my tyrant
without altering pace—in fact pretending to ignore
his existence.   I don't mean to say I felt happy in
my mind—the ground was open, not a semblance of
a bush round which to dodge him had he carried
out his amiable intentions to the full—all that
could be done was to take things quietly.   I looked
round ; the brute was following at a walk, but
getting over the brow of a rise I clapped spurs and
—went ; so when my pursuer's objectionable proportions appeared against the sky line, I had put
such a distance between us as to have the laugh
entirely on my own side.

After a ride of several hours I found the
waggon outspanned on a high ridge opposite
Intaba'nkulu, a long flat-topped mountain some
twenty miles from Inhlazatye.   Some of the people

from neighbouring kraals paid me a visit, and sat talking as usual about the war and Cetywayo; several had snuffboxes stuck in their ears, consisting of revolver cartridge cases with stoppers, which they said they had picked up at Isandhlwana. In the middle of the day three Zulus carrying bundles of assegais went by in rather a hurried manner; however, thinking to trade for an assegai or two, I called out to them to stop. They came up, but would hardly sit down. ' What was the news?' I asked, seeing that something was in the wind. They replied that Ndabuku had gone to Maritzburg after the Resident, because Sibepu was sending a force against him to ' eat him up.' Then gathering up their assegais they started off at a rapid pace, saying they could not wait any longer.

The above intelligence, if true, most likely pointed to a row, Ndabuku and Mnyamane being the prime agitators and leaders of the King's party, as against Sibepu, John Dunn, and Uhamu; and the fact of Ndabuku having gone into Natal would show that something was brewing. I had noticed a good deal of unrest among the people in different parts of the country, and now I was in one of the most disturbed centres.

But meanwhile the weather, which had brightened up since the morning, again became gloomy

and threatening; a dark cloud working up from
the south-west, and a distant flash and faint roll of
thunder, warned me what to expect. Gradually a
black pall spread from the horizon till nearly overhead; from my elevated position I overlooked the
country for miles, and near and far huge dark
columns were moving along as heavy showers
swept over the plain. Louder and nearer came
each successive roll, and bright jets rent the inky
cloud into many a ragged edge. There is something very awe-inspiring about the approach of a
storm in these regions. The wildness of the surroundings; the boding stillness that falls upon all
nature; the towering ruggedness of the mountains;
the vastness of the bare spreading plains, over
which the huge curtain, black as night, comes
sweeping up, like the slow and sure advance of
some fell host from whose pursuit there is no
escape; and the ground trembles beneath the
long, deep, threatening roll, and a scorching smell
fills the air as each blue steely jet strikes down into
the very earth. A crash which seems to split the
mountain tops asunder has scarcely time to die
away in reverberating roar among the crags, when
another, yet more startling in its appalling sudden-
ness, follows upon it, while the fluid plays around in
vivid streams; and stunned and deafened by the
terrific din and well-nigh blinded by the dazzling

glare, you feel as though enveloped in a sheet of electric flame.

We hastened to inspan, thinking to avoid the storm, or at any rate to get into a better place, but had not gone far before it became necessary to halt. There were some kraals lying on the plain, nor was it long before one of their inhabitants came to see who I was, and pointed out the way to Hlobane, saying I could get there next day. He said that Uhamu [1] had been ' eating up ' and killing numbers of people all round Hlobane, and that the Abaqulusi section, to which he (my informant) belonged, had been driven out altogether, but he had heard that some of them had gone back. He didn't seem to consider himself safe even there, for although now in Tyingwayo's territory, yet Tyingwayo was a friend of Mnyamane, who was for the King, and an *impi* might arrive from Uhamu at any moment. However, I induced him to go a little way with me, the track being somewhat indistinct, and the storm having cleared away we started. After about an hour's travelling I parted with my guide, and struck into the valley which skirts the northern side of Intaba'nkulu.

---

[1] A half-brother of Cetywayo's, commonly, but erroneously, known as Oham, who came over to the British side shortly after the commencement of hostilities. He was appointed under the Ulundi settlement to a district in Northern Zululand, but has the reputation of being rather a tyrant.

For a little while after sundown the sky kept clear enough, and one could see the way, albeit the same was very bad and swampy, but this was not to last, for now heavy clouds began to work up, speedily obscuring the moon. The track went from bad to worse ; at times one would have to stop and go on hands and knees, literally to 'nose' out where it lay, and no sooner fairly on the move again than the wheel would sink to the axle in a mudhole. Outspanning was not to be thought of ; we were in the middle of a regular swamp, and must get through somehow ; but get through we must, as to that there could be no mistake whatever. It became darker and darker, above on either side loomed the mountains, the harsh croaking of innumerable reptiles sounded from the slimy morass, while every now and then a ghostly blue light would flicker and disappear, to gleam out again a few yards further. Splash, splash—on we went, the ground wet and glistening as we ploughed through it ; not a yard of the way did any one of us know, and it was a case of forging ahead and trusting to Providence. Cheerful position ! A dreary swamp towards midnight in a gloomy defile in the heart of a wild country ; the track scarce discernible, and a thunderstorm rolling up behind, for by that time there was every promise of a repetition of the midday entertainment. A heavy shower or two would reduce the ground to an impassable state, it might be for days. The idea acted like a spur; we pushed on with re-doubled energy. Now one wheel would plunge into a hole, or both would stick fast in a narrow but deep runnel, to be extracted therefrom with much holloaing and cracking of whip; then we would get off the track, and only find it again with some difficulty and considerable delay. But at last the ground became firmer, the clouds parted a little, and the moon shone out—the worst was over, and after crossing a shallow river which ran plashing and bubbling in the moonlight, we camped for the rest of the night; none too soon either, for the rain came down smartly, and the storm which had been following us now burst. But thoroughly tired out, I dropped off to sleep in the middle of it.

The next morning was cool, not to say chilly, and though masses of cloud were hanging about and drifting slowly apart, there seemed no proba-bility of more rain. I found that we were in one of those basin-like valleys which form a special feature in that part of the country, and as the team laboured slowly up the steep road I was able to take in the scene of our nocturnal march; then as we ascended higher and higher Intaba'nkulu was left behind.

We move along beneath the bush-clad heights
—one wooded peak standing out above the rest
against the sky—poised over many a circular
kraal with which the deep narrow valley below is
studded. Rivulets leap from rock to rock, burying themselves in the mossy recesses of their
funnel-like beds, to emerge with a dash and sparkle,
and plunge on laughing over their slippery stones ;
feathery tree ferns wave their fanlike boughs above
the path ; and at last we gain the ridge. A fresh
view opens out, and we look down upon the bare
treeless plains lying beneath the rugged precipitous
range comprising Zunguin and Hlobane of ill-
starred fame.

CHAPTER XVII

A WILD waste, flat and treeless; grey clouds thickly
veil the sky, and the shades of evening are fast
gathering. In front, like a wall, rises the side of
a long hill; no kraals or grazing herds upon its
dark slope lend life to its desolation; no break
occurs in the hard, regular line of perpendicular
rock wherewith its summit is crowned—a stern and
forbidding height. This is Hlobane mountain.

We cross a reedy swamp lying in a hollow of
the plain, whose slimy pools resound with the
croaking of frogs and the splash of reptiles as they
plunge into the muddy depths, and wind along a
level flat. The marsh just left is the source of the
Black Umfolosi. Skirting the base of the Hlobane
we pass a high conical hill called Nyambi, which
rises on our left front, and by the time we are
camped opposite the ridge connecting Hlobane with
Entendeke, night has long since set in. The posi-

tion is a lonely one, and seems none the less so that every yard we have traversed in order to reach it has been *terra incognita*. Southward, among heavy piles of clouds, lightning gleams are ever and anon playing, the shadowy outline of Hlobane looms above, while half-way up the Zunguin a grass fire glows red against the pitchy blackness.

In the morning I find that there are several kraals in the neighbourhood, some of whose occupants are not slow to look me up, and I take the opportunity of compassing a guide in order to make the ascent. A young Zulu, who had taken part in the fight, volunteers, and we start. Hlobane rises to a height of about 1,000 feet from the plain ; its summit, some three miles in length, is in the shape of an irregular lozenge, whose western point connects by a high razor-like ridge with Entendeke, a steep table topped mountain. With horses it can only be ascended on the eastern side, to wit, that farthest from Kambúla, and at one point on the southern, which I chose as being nearest my camp.

What a climb it is ! A narrow zigzag cattle path hollowed into holes, or with huge stones to be got over like so many steps in a flight of stairs. And steep—it is like making the ascent of a high-pitched roof. Riding is out of the question most of the way, so I resign my pony to Andries, who, poor fellow, is puffing and blowing like a traction engine. The guide, however, doesn't seem to mind it at all, skipping merrily from stone to stone, as if swarming up a thousand feet of nearly perpendicular ascent were the most enjoyable of recreations ; he grins and shows all his white teeth gleefully, as from the top of a rock he surveys my distressful and perspiring countenance, and chucks me one of his kerries to aid my efforts. But everything comes to an end, and so, eventually, does our climb, and we find ourselves on the summit, which is quite flat, with a stream of clear water running right across it.

Hlobane is totally unlike any of the adjacent mountains ; its steep slopes culminate in a belt of sheer cliff round whose base rocks and boulders lie piled in rugged confusion, giving the idea that at some time or other the top of the mountain has fallen away all round, as indeed must have been the case. Many of these rocks are of enormous size, and it was among the holes and caves formed by them that the Zulus lay in wait for our men when they stormed the mountain. Beneath the southern cliff is the site of one of Umbelini's strongholds, with part of the wall of the cattle enclosure still standing, and from his eyrie-like position that bold marauder commanded a view of the tract below. From the eastern side I could make out a white cross on the slope beneath, the grave of some victim of the fatal day. All too sadly frequent are these monuments in the wilderness.

The Zulus whom I found at the waggon on my return had all taken part in the fight, and their account of it was briefly this :—About the middle of the morning a British force arrived from Kambúla camp and reconnoitred round the mountain, looking for a place whereby to effect an ascent. The Zulus at the top, consisting of Umbelini's men and the Abaqulusi (to which clan my informants belonged) were carefully watching the horsemen, and being pretty sure that the west side of the mountain would be the one attacked, lost no time in getting into position among the caves. It was no use ; they shot one or two of the officers, but the British pressed on, dislodging them, and, gaining the summit, drove them into cover among the rocks at the sides. They could not tell the time about, for it was a rainy day and the sun not visible, but it must have been late in the afternoon when an *impi* appeared on the opposite hills. When the Zulus on the mountain saw the *impi* they stole round behind the British so as to cut off their retreat, whereupon these made for the western point, and the Zulus charging in upon them from behind, drove them towards Entendeke. I have

said that the latter was connected with Hlobane
by a narrow ridge, but to reach this about a hundred feet of steep precipitous ground has to be
got over—a regular drop—a place that no one
would dream of riding down in cold blood. Down
it, then, however, our men had to go, the savages
charging them with fierce shouts, terrifying to
madness the already frightened horses, many of
which, losing their foothold, rolled over and over
down the fearful declivity. Other Zulus swarmed
round the bases of the western cliffs to cut off the
fugitives, who were flying in the utmost disorder,
some mounted, others on foot, and meanwhile that
terrible legion was sweeping across the plain,
thousands and thousands of relentless foes, advancing rapidly and surely, utterly to annihilate
the whole reconnoitring party. Many of these
were killed among the boulders on Hlobane,
others on the ridge, while others again, who were
unhorsed, were cut off on the plain beneath. The
fugitives, mounted and on foot, made for Kambúla
camp, distant across country some twelve or
fifteen miles. 'A great many were killed,' concluded my informant, ' on the flats along the base
of the Zunguin, and not until dark did the pursuit
cease.'

I asked them about Grandier, the Frenchman
who was supposed to have been captured during

the retreat from Hlobane, and to have escaped by killing one of his guards while being taken to Umbelini's clan for execution. They said that a white man had been taken prisoner and brought to Ulundi; that Cetywayo had questioned him, and had then sent him back under an escort, with orders that he should be let go near Hlobane, so that he could find his way to the English camp, but they knew nothing about the killing of the guard. Their statement agreed with that of other Zulus whom I interrogated on the subject in various parts of the country.

There are improbabilities about the Frenchman's story which certainly seem to need accounting for. His escape was avowedly made during the halt after the first march, to wit, within a few miles of Ulundi. But in that case it would not take long for the surviving guard to return at full speed and raise the country on the fugitive's heels, whose recapture would be but a question of a very few hours. Then, again, from Ulundi to the Zunguin, where Grandier was picked up, is a little matter of fifty miles as the crow flies, and a good deal more by any known track; further, it is extremely rugged and mountainous, as the foregoing pages may have served to show. How, then, could this man, on foot and without food, find his way across an unknown wilderness, exposed, as he would be, to the glance of Zulu scouting parties patrolling the hills ? On the other hand, it may fairly be asked what motive would Cetywayo have for sparing the life of a prisoner— an unusual act of leniency on the part of a savage chief—exasperated too, as he would naturally be, by the defeat of his forces at Kambúla and the loss of hundreds of his best warriors. Unless it were that the King had heard how some Zulu prisoners had been tended by our surgeons, or, with a desperate sense of his ultimate downfall coming more and more home to him, thought by this act of clemency to commend himself more readily to our sympathies when his day came, and take a step in the direction of agreeing with his adversary quickly. Again, should Grandier's narrative be correct in every particular, it might be that the survivor of the two men who guarded him, fearing to go back and tell the King how ill he had acquitted himself of his charge, had simply made himself scarce and said nothing, which would account for the Frenchman not being recaptured. But whatever may be thought of the tale, the Zulus all agree that the King's orders were for the release of the captive.

While camped beneath Hlobane I would frequently roam about alone, exploring its rugged fastnesses. One evening, when scrambling up an

exceptionally stony path, momentarily expecting
to be obliged to turn back, a sudden start and a
snort from my pony caused me to look up.
Within a few yards, leaning against a rock, stood a
couple of stalwart savages calmly watching me. I
saw that one of them carried an assegai with a
blade like a small claymore, and, seeing, coveted
and resolved to have it if possible. I climbed to
where they stood; the warriors greeted me as
usual, ' Inkos! ' and of course were anxious to
know all about me. The one with the assegai was
a fine, tall fellow, with a cheery countenance and
hearty manner, and we speedily became friends;
the other, dark, taciturn, and unprepossessing, I
didn't much like the look of. But he of the
assegai did his companion's share of *indaba* and
his own too. He belonged to the Udhloko regiment, and had been present at the attack on Rorke's
Drift, which battle he proceeded to fight over
again for my enlightenment with an effusiveness
and pantomimic accompaniment thoroughly Zulu;
going into fits of laughter over it, as though one of
the toughest struggles on record were the greatest
joke in the world. At a judicious moment I produced some ' gwai,' which was received with
acclamation, even my saturnine friend's dark
countenance expanding into a grin. Then taking
up the assegai I began to examine it, suggesting

that we should make an exchange, and throwing out all sorts of inducements. Not a bit of it; the jovial warrior would about as soon think of parting with his head-ring—or his head. He had fought with that very weapon 'kwa Jim' (Rorke's Drift) &c. &c. ; no, he couldn't give it away on any account. It was a splendid specimen of a spear, but on no terms could I obtain it.

The sun had gone down, the hush of evening had fallen upon the lone mountain side and upon the dark forms of the two Zulus where they stood among the grey rocks, while a few yards beneath, my horse, saddled and bridled, was quietly cropping the short grass which sprouted up between the stones. And in thorough keeping with the surroundings was the tall lithe figure of the savage standing on the stony ledge in relief against the sky, and, as he narrated some incident, waving an arm with graceful gesture over the panorama of plain and mountain rolling away into the far distance. As we stood there in friendly converse, representatives of the two nations, civilised and barbarous, who had fought so fiercely and poured each other's blood like water upon the rugged sides of this very mountain, I longed for the limner's art that I might place the scene upon canvas there and then. The darkness crept on apace; dimly faded the cliffs above into shadowy gloom, and far

away upon the plain beneath, the tent of my
waggon was just visible like a white speck. And
now my friend who had done all the talking
signified his intention of going home ; so picking
up his assegai he strode off with a cheery farewell,
followed by his companion. A light shone forth
on the mountain side a little way off, where, perched
eyrie-like on a kind of ledge, stood a small kraal
consisting of three or four huts, and I could see
the brown figures of the two Zulus making their
way thither among the rocks and long grass.

Before leaving Hlobane I wanted thoroughly
to explore the line of retreat, so starting the
waggon early one morning on the road to Kambúla,
I rode off alone with that intent. Skirting the
Entendeke I worked round to the western side and
began the ascent, which was very like that already
described, except that it made up in steepness for
not being so stony ; in some places the horse could
barely keep his feet, and I expected every moment
to see him roll over. On, higher and higher, up a
stony gully rendered slippery by the trickle of a
thread of water. Here I picked up an ordinary
metal button half embedded in the soil, but of
other relics I found none, though on the look-out
for them ; and at last after a toilsome and dangerous climb—even a sprained ankle in that out-of-
the-way place assumes serious proportions, and

precipices abound—I reached the top, and cantering along its smooth level stood upon the narrow ridge. Looking at the piles of rocks and boulders leading up to the summit of Hlobane, full well could I realise the utter confusion which must have characterised the rush of a crowd of horsemen down that fearful place. Nor when they gained the ridge would things be much better, for over and above its narrowness and the almost precipitous slopes on either side, it is stony to a degree, and many a dangerous crevice lies hidden away in the long grass. A cairn of loose stones on the ridge marks the spot where the brave old Dutch commandant, Piet Uys, fell.

Something of indescribable desolation seemed to haunt the place, as though one were standing alone outside the world. Heavy clouds were gathering in the west, and the morning breeze came in fitful puffs, singing through the long grass as through the strings of a harp, then leaving a stillness as of death. Directly opposite towered Zunguin's lofty head, huge and sullen; while the northern slope of Hlobane fell in one bold sweep a descent of more than a thousand feet, and the eye wandered over savage ravines and frowning krantzes farther and farther to many a distant peak in the Transvaal and Swaziland. Far away I could see my waggon with its twelve black oxen, crawling along like a centipede, but not a sound came up to that silent ledge, poised, as it were, between earth and heaven, the abode of an almost supernatural stillness.   As I turned to follow the line of flight, I thought how small were the odds in favour of those who had to race for their lives, with the dark sweeping mass moving so swiftly over the plain to cut off their retreat.   The summit of Entendeke is smooth enough, which may have had something to do with affording the fugitives a start upon beginning their hard race ; once over the brow the trial begins.   In cold blood the descent was difficult enough ; the sides were like glass, and one would slip and slide perhaps a dozen yards before able to pull up, at imminent peril of being shot over one of the many precipices which break the continuity of the slopes.   But the idea of charging blindly down at breakneck pace made one shudder. At last I stood beneath, on Zunguin's Neck, myself and steed uninjured, but not half sorry to be down again, and considerably out of breath after the climb and the descent.

CHAPTER XVIII

A 'stick,' but in the mud—'Dutch spoken here'—'Philip drunk'—
More rain—A Republican—Kambúla—Zulu account of the battle
—Relics—A cemetery in the wilderness—Back to the border.

KAMBULA is, as before stated, about fifteen miles
from Hlobane across country, but by road nearly
double that distance. I ride along the base of the
desolate Zunguin range ; here and there a swamp
has to be crossed or a détour made to avoid a long
reach of water ; twice having cleared a deep
runnel my pony sinks to his knees on the brink in
the boggy, treacherous soil, nearly pitching me
over his head ; but the game little rascal scrambles
through—as what will a Basuto pony not scramble through ?—and we hold on our way. Past
Seketwayo's kraal, lying there at the base of the
mountain, which chief, though ruler of one of the
districts and a man of rank and lineage, is not an
interesting person, and to tell the truth I am getting just a little anxious to take the homeward
track again ; wherefore I deny myself the pleasure

of looking him up, and keep straight on till I over-take the waggon.   That trusty vehicle, however, is at a standstill, both front wheels sticking hard and fast in a swampy runnel, while a little old Zulu with an enormous assegai stands placidly contem-plating the joint efforts of its three perspiring guardians to effect an extraction.   In vain does Fani brandish his long whip and execute a series of appalling 'cracks,' in vain does Mlamvu tug doggedly and despairingly at the leading 'touw,' in vain do Fani and Andries combine in calling down dire maledictions on the horned heads of 'Windvogel,' and 'Bckvel,' and 'Kwaaiman,' and 'Mof,' and threaten those longsuffering animals with magnified extermination—they, in common with their brethren in the yoke, are doing their level best and can do no more—the wheels remain fast embedded in the black sticky earth.   Unlash-ing the spade and pick, we dig away furiously for a space, thus affording a short rest to the panting span as well as smoothing the way.   Crack, crack—goes the whip ; we yell frantically in chorus ; 'a long, long pull, and a strong, strong pull,' the machine sways and jolts, and emerges uninjured ; the little old Zulu, thinking there is no more to be seen, trots off on his way, and we resume ours.

But now we are getting into the 'Disputed

Territory,'[1] and signs of Dutch vicinity may be detected in the phraseology of the natives. The old familiar greeting, 'Inkos!' ringing out, with the poetry of the wilderness about it, changes to the common-place and low-sounding 'Moro Baas' (Good morning, Master); now and then 'Ja' takes the place of the emphatic 'Ehé!' and enterprising individuals even try their hand at Dutch colloquy. We pass between several kraals; outside of one stands a ramshackle cart containing the wares of some half-caste Dutch trader, the beneficial results of whose mission soon manifest themselves in the shape of a couple of tall, savage-looking Zulus, both extremely drunk, who reel up to the waggon boisterously demanding all sorts of things. With the greatest difficulty do we keep them from tumbling under the wheels as they stagger alongside, and at last, to get rid of them, I chuck them a box of matches, which has the desired effect, and, quite pleased, the fellows roll back to their kraal, to absorb more alcohol and probably to finish by breaking each other's heads and those of their neighbours— unfortunately, not the trader's.

We outspanned that night at what is known as the Old Hunting Road. A grey mist had settled

---

[1] A strip of country on the Transvaal border, between the Pongolo and the Blood River, claimed by the Boers, but awarded to the Zulus by the Boundary Commission which sat at Rorke's Drift in February 1878.

down upon the land, and a chill wind blew in violent gusts ; the firewood, having been wetted by a
shower during the day, declined to ignite ; then,
to crown all, with scarcely any warning a violent
thunderstorm broke over us, and in ten minutes'
time every pot and kettle was in requisition to
catch the leakages through the waggon tent : fire
being out of the question in the drenching rain
which ploughed up the road into a very morass.

Morning dawned on the far from cheerful
scene ; the rain had ceased, but heavy fog still
hung in masses about the hills ; there was no sign
of the sun, and it behoved us to wait for the ground
to dry a little before resuming progress. While
sitting on the waggon box smoking the pipe of
patience, I descried a horseman coming up the road
—travellers had hitherto been like the proverbial
angelic visitations, few and far between, wherefore I inspected this one with some curiosity as he
reined in. He was a rather respectable-looking
Dutchman, grey bearded and chimney-pot hatted ;
moreover spoke English well. Now the Boer as a
rule is modest in the display of linguistic attain-
ments even if possessed of any, in fact does not
attempt the English tongue unless he be—to use a
nautical phrase—' three sheets in the wind ; ' even
then his performance is an indifferent one. But in
this instance my friend was eminently sober, and

talked the Queen's English rather fluently. I began to suspect I had to do with some Transvaal magnate, the more so that he seemed anxious to get upon the topic of the late rebellion, saying that he had fought on the side of ' the Republic.'

' Didn't I think the whole affair had been a great mistake ? '

' Yes, I rather thought it had.'

At this my friend became quite animated, and after some more talk on the subject, appealingly asked whether I was of opinion that we should be any the better for the possession of the Transvaal. I stood up and looked round for a minute upon the bare, treeless wastes, the desolate ranges and dark sad peaks northward, and was able conscientiously to reply in the negative. Whereat my interlocutor seemed puzzled whether to look disappointed or pleased ; I think the former sentiment predominated, for he almost immediately took his leave. He told me his name, which I have forgotten, but it was not one of any note.

The road being dry enough for a move, a short *trek* brought us to Kambúla, where we outspanned within a hundred yards of the old fort.

I said that the surroundings were dismal, and verily nothing could have been more cheerless than the outlook, as, swathed in a mackintosh, I explored the site of the fort and laager amid a chilling and

continuous drizzle.　But its unexhilarating entour-
age notwithstanding, Kambúla camp was about
the best for defensive purposes I had seen in Zululand.　It consisted of two *laagers* and a fort—
forming an obtuse-angled triangle, the three posi-
tions being from two to three hundred yards apart.
The fort occupied the highest and central point of
the ridge, the two *laagers* being situated one on
each side in such wise that they commanded a slope
all round.　The front is the worst side, as the
ground falls suddenly away at a distance of about
three hundred yards from the position ; in the rear
is a long gradual slope.　About a mile off, a desolate range of hills shuts in the view on the right
front, but to the left the country is open and undulating, and it was from this direction that the
impi first appeared.　Intense must have been the
expectation and excitement among the defenders
as, for hours before the attack, they watched the
dark masses deploying over the plain, marching
steadily on, no thought of wavering in their fell
purpose.　And still they kept appearing, column
after column, till the earth was black ; and our
men would soon have an opportunity of avenging
the previous day's disaster, or—not one would live
to bear away the tale of this ; for in the event of
defeat no mercy need be looked for from yon cloud
of threatening savages sweeping along, stern and

intrepid, to annihilate the hated invader. On they came, chanting a war-song in vaunt of what they had done at Isandhlwana and would do again.

And throughout that long afternoon amid the smoke and din ; the screech of shell and rattle of volleys ; the deep-toned war-shout mingling with the scarcely less wild British cheer ; the thunderous tread of the charging myriads as again and again they surged up the incline, again and again to fall back leaving the gory slope strewn with writhing bodies—throughout that long afternoon the fate of our countrymen hung in the balance. But what could savages, however brave and well organised, effect against such a position, so staunchly defended, and with all the latest appliances, too, of nineteenth century warfare. They wavered and fled, and the previous day's disaster was amply wiped out by the utter dispersion of the flower of the martial strength of Zululand, which, leaving more than 1,000 of its bravest warriors dead around the British camp, must now go back to its King shamed and defeated, by that very circumstance warning him of his approaching downfall.

The following is the narrative of a warrior of the Tulwana regiment, a division of the Undi :—

' Two days before the affair at Hlobane we

started from Undini; the King himself arranged the plan of attack and position of the regiments. When we arrived near Hlobane we heard firing and saw a number of white men fighting with the Abaqulusi on the mountain. They retreated as we advanced, but a great many were killed. We slept that night at Hlobane, marching on Kambúla the next day. The regiments were the Undi, Udhloko, Nokenke, Umpunga, Nodwengu, Kandampemvu (Umcityu), Umbonambi, and Ngobamakosi; this last led the right "horn." The *izinduna* present were Tyingwayo, Mnyamane, Sirayo, Mavumengwane, Mundúla and Matyana-ka-Mondisi; they watched the fight from a hill (about three miles off). When we got near the camp some horsemen came out to meet us. Then the Ngobamakosi rushed after them; they retreated, and the Ngobamakosi in following them got quite separated from the main body of the *impi*. Then the Kandampemvu on the other side rushed on, too—there was a rivalry between the Kandampemvu and the Ngobamakosi as to who should be first in camp, so they both got on ahead, and by the time we came up to attack in front they were exhausted and almost beaten. The Undi managed to get into the cattle-laager, but were driven out again. We could not stand against the fire and had to retreat; the two regiments forming the

" horns " were quite exhausted and useless, and we could not properly surround the position.

'We were in smaller force than at Isandhlwana, but were sure of being able to " eat up " the English ; as it is we should have done so, had not the Ngobamakosi and the Kandampemvu acted like fools. The King was very angry when we went back ; he said we were born warriors, and yet allowed ourselves to be defeated in every battle, and soon the English would come and take *him*. We lost far more men at Kambúla than at Isandhlwana.'

The tumbledown wall and crumbling earthwork of the fort still crests the mound : of the two laagers one is overgrown with a crop of mealies, the other is plainly to be traced by the tent marks and scattered débris. I picked up an old gun-barrel, and a button-cleaner belonging to the 13th Regiment ; bullets, too, and plenty of exploded cartridge cases lay about. On the north of the camp is a little cemetery where rest the remains of those who fell ; the central monument, a stone cross, standing a conspicuous object against the surrounding waste. This enclosure is under the care of an old Zulu, who showed me his credentials from Sir Evelyn Wood, and was anxious for me to inspect the place and report well thereon. As a matter of fact it was in very good order: in one corner the remnant of recent showers still lay, which, when I pointed out, the old fellow started off there and then for a spade and proceeded to cut a drain through the sod wall. Further down the slope, three or four dark spots of a different growth show the places of sepulture of the Zulu dead, who were buried in hundreds after the battle.

And now, having thoroughly explored the camp and its surroundings, I find there is nothing more to be done but to start for home; and, as I said before, Kambúla is not an exhilarating spot. Wherefore we inspan and roll into the road again, having made the round of the country and 'done' all the battlefields in succession, of which this is the last.

Very few days now will bring us to the border; the spirits of my 'boys' rise; even the oxen seem to know they are bound for home, and step out briskly as we hold steadily on over a bare desolate waste where the great hills with their rock-crowned summits are sleeping in their solitude. On past Bemba's Kop and along the Blood river, and away to the left rises the Munhla hill; then, as we near Itelezi, the square huts, flocks of goats, and mounted natives show that we are among Hlubi's Basutos. Then, one morning we halt on the Emponjane ridge. There, in front, some twelve

miles off, rise the blue gum trees at Rorke's Drift
house, beneath the Shiyane hill; while nearer, are
the buildings of St. Augustine's Mission and Hlubi's
domicile. A cheer breaks from my trusty followers,
who are elate at the prospect of being speedily at
home again; nor am I disinclined to sympathise, for
we have had a good spell of the rough and tumble
of daily travel, and a little rest and civilisation will
not come amiss.

We reach St. Augustine's in the afternoon:
bidding farewell to the hospitable missionary, I
start the waggon with orders to outspan on the
other side of Rorke's Drift, while I ride round by
Isandhlwana to pick up the post—if haply there
be any—and take leave of the Bishop and his
community, to whom, in memory of much kind-
ness and of pleasant days, I here take the opportunity of wishing all success.

The following day I cross the Buffalo and am
in Natal again; and as we move along the border
on the road to Helpmakaar (a different one this
time), and the evening sun throws his beams full
upon the rocky face of Isandhlwana, which is fading
smaller and smaller behind us, and lights up with
a golden lustre the broad rolling plains and the
winding river, I must plead guilty to experiencing
a tinge of regret that never again shall I wander
through that fair land—never again hold pleasant

converse with its warrior denizens, so intrepid in defence of their country, so kindly and open-hearted now that the dark cloud of war has lifted and the red wave has flowed on.

Next morning we reach Helpmakaar without event. One more glimpse of the Zulu border, and we descend the heights of the Biggarsberg to Umsinga.

CHAPTER XIX

A panorama—Zulu dances—A bushbuck 'drive'—Native hunters—
Return to Maritzburg—Afloat again.

BEING in Zululand for purposes of travel I did
not lay myself out at all for sport, having no dogs
for bird shooting, and bush-hunting necessitates a
regular 'drive,' which takes time and a little
trouble to organise ; but I had an opportunity of
seeing something in this line before ending my
wanderings, for a border friend was kind enough
to get up a bushbuck hunt on my account. He
had several trading stores planted along the border, and to one of these we were to proceed, having
sent up everything requisite and necessary for
making a night of it.

Behold us then, four in all, mounted and ready
for a start ; and before the sun has time to make
his power felt, we are cantering along the grassy
flats towards the mountains. Our horses pick their
way gingerly across a broad slab of slippery rock,
over which the water, trickling, falls into a clear
pool fringed with delicate mosses and sparkling

ferns, and we enter a steep winding bush-path :
mimosa branches with their sharp thorns sweep
across the saddle, aloes stand about the hill side
like black sentinels, and from the plumed euphorbia the turtle-dove suddenly stops her melodious ' cooing ' to dash away in a flutter of alarm
at the advent of the—shall I say it ?—somewhat
noisy group now breaking in upon the sleepy
stillness of Nature.   We come to a native kraal in
a little hollow, whose inhabitants with their curs
turn out to inspect us.   ' Now then, you fellows,'
sings out my friend, ' tumble out and go on up
and help drive; we've sent up a cow for you to
kill to-night when it's all over.'   ' Yeh-bo'nkos ! '
they reply vociferously, for the prospect of a good
bush hunt culminating in beef and jollification is
more than the aboriginal mind can resist ; so,
diving into the huts, the jovial barbarians soon
reappear with assegais and shields, and, with their
curs at their heels, start off gleefully for the scene
of operations.   We pass other kraals, whose
occupants are already on the move and preparing
to follow in the ruck ; more and more stony becomes the path, and steeper withal, till at last we
have to dismount and lead our steeds.   But we
will pause here for a moment and look around.
There is the Biggarsberg range, at whose base the
roofs of the public offices and Sand Spruit buildings

show out against the plain. Yonder, the huge
cone of Elénge towers above the surrounding
heights; far beneath, the Tugela is winding like a
serpent through its deep wild valley; and many a
lofty mountain heaves its bare head to the sky,
its wooded sides falling in abrupt sweeps, to lose
themselves in the vast sea of forest, which, undulating in mighty waves of slope and ravine, now
gentle, now bold and forbidding, stretches, far as
the eye can reach, into misty dimness. Here a
huge krantz rears its frowning wall; there a mighty
rock, which, detaching itself from some overhanging
cliff, has rolled down, and now lies firmly embedded
in the midst of the bush. Here and there, in a
small cleared space, stands a native kraal with its
quaint circle of huts; and the eye ranges at will,
far and wide, over the roll of mountain and valley
and plain to the lofty peaks of distant Kahlamba
looming in shadowy outline through the soft haze.
And standing thus in the golden sunshine and warm
air, it strikes me that a more gloriously magnificent
panorama would be difficult to find.

But forward—so cresting the brow of the
height we turn our backs upon the splendid scene
and gallop over the wide grassy plains opening out
in front, along which at intervals may be seen a
line of natives in twos and threes, mounted and
afoot, all making in the same direction. Another

hour's ride and we draw up at a small rough-looking building standing at the head of a valley, affording a picturesque peep of the Tugela winding through the bush beneath ; while immediately around, the broad green leaves and waving plumes of standing corn rustle in the breeze.   This is the place of rendezvous.   The house, which is a trading store, has two rooms, one being fitted up with counter, shelves, &c., such as I have already described earlier in this narrative ; the other apparently doing duty as kitchen, larder, and bed-room put together, for the half of a buck hangs in front of the fireplace, and a ' stretcher ' stands against the wall on one side of the apartment.

We dismount ; crowds of natives are standing, sitting, and lolling about in every conceivable attitude, talking, chattering, and laughing, in fact kicking up an indescribable and deafening shindy ; dogs sneak in and out, getting into everyone's way and being kicked and yelling accordingly.   Plenty of these are there, by the way ; curs black, brown, and grey ;   curs white and curs brindled ; in short, curs of every shade and colour.   The Zulu dogs are mostly a kind of greyhound or lurcher ; in the bush they will run down anything previously wounded, but for speed are nowhere.

I am introduced to the chief, a stout pleasant-looking man rejoicing in the name of Mawéle, with

whom my friend seems to be on the best possible
terms.   Presently an unmistakable sound is heard,
and lo, a fresh body of natives, some fifty strong,
appears, marching in a square and singing a war
song ; the suppressed fierceness of the strange
wild chant forming a perfect accompaniment to
the rattle of assegais and shields and the measured
tread of many feet.   They file into the open space,
stand motionless for a moment, and at a sign
from their leader fall out and disperse.

But it is too soon to start yet, and to while
away the time the natives get up a dance.   They
stand in a semicircle several ranks deep, with their
shields and knob-kerries, the master of ceremonies
with his small white shield in front.   He gives the
signal; a kind of weird quartet is heard in the ranks,
first very softly, then taken up by one after another, but still softly, all keeping time with their
feet ; presently it grows louder and louder, and the
whole crowd seems labouring under the intensest
of suppressed excitement.   They turn themselves
half round, first to this side, then to that, but
never budging an inch from their places, and the
earth shakes beneath the thunder of their feet as
they bring them to the ground like one man.
They clash their knob-kerries and shields together ;
they roar like wild beasts ; but never for a moment
do you lose the modulation of the fantastic

harmony, the rhythm of the strange, fierce, thrilling chant to which you feel yourself unconsciously beating time ; and an irresistible longing comes over you to seize a kerrie, throw yourself into the rout, and stamp and howl with the best of them.

The ground is quivering beneath the tread of many feet, eyeballs gleam and start from their sockets, the clash of knob-kerries and shields is deafening, the hill tops echo back the savage fury of the unearthly chant, the excitement is wrought to the highest pitch, when—the master of ceremonies gives a slight signal, and the whole of that frenzied crowd becomes still and motionless as statues. A few minutes of rest, of panting and blowing after the violent exertion, and the sign is given. Again the ' choragi' lead off, the crowd takes up another song, and the fun waxes fast and furious till the word goes forth to prepare for a start. Assegais and kerries are collected, among much clatter ; dogs, nosing out their owners, fall in behind them ; and all move off. Some of the Zulus form up into companies and march for the scene of operations humming a hunting song ; others go off by twos and threes to their assigned places, and mounting our horses we make for where we shall get the best chance of a shot and see most of the drive, for the natives have no idea of our having all the sport to ourselves.

A short ride brings us to a grassy 'neck;' in front lies a wide bush-covered valley, and round the hillside on our right a growing clamour points to the approach of the beaters. Far away on the other side of the bush can be seen the dark forms of the native hunters drawing in their line and working up towards us, while eager groups stand ready with assegai and kerrie. A rush, a shout, and a prolonged yell from the curs—a buck is up and away, and we can trace his course by the agitation among the bush beneath as he springs through it. Those who have rifles—it is too far for shot guns—make for a point commanding an open space which the quarry must cross. Bang, bang!—a cloud of dust flies round the startled antelope; it was a near shave. Bang!—again the dust rises behind him, but he is in the thick bush, and safe ; and a string of dogs, black, brown, and grey, crosses the open, yelling like fiends, on his track. But the sight of quarry has roused the latent instinct of destruction in Briton and native alike, and we are all tenfold on the *qui vive*. The hunt sweeps on ; hark!—a warning shout. Look at those two Zulus down there, how they listen for a moment and run forward noiselessly as shadows. They stand, eyeballs starting and nostrils dilated, in an attitude of intense expectancy, still, motionless like bronze statues, one foot advanced, head and shoulders bent forward in a panther-like crouch, in the right hand a long tapering assegai. Nearer and nearer comes the crashing of the under-wood, the bushes part, and a graceful form leaps lightly into the glade within a few yards of them. It is a young bushbuck ram, and the sun glints on the points of his shiny black horns and lustrous eye as he catches sight of his human foes, and, with a frightened start, leaps off at a tangent. Well for him that he does, or he would at this moment be lying transfixed in his death throes, for the murderous spear grazes his shoulder as he turns, and the blade sticks quivering in the ground. Zip !—another assegai flashes through the air, and the ill-fated antelope plunges and rolls over and over. The two Zulus raise an exultant whoop, but no, not yet ; he is up again, and whisking his white tail defiantly, bounds safe into the friendly bush. But he is hard hit and will not go far. Dogs are called, and the two Zulus, stooping to pick up the gore-stained assegai, dash into the bush on the heels of the pack. A yell—a chorus of clamour—a scream—as the bloodthirsty curs throw themselves upon their quarry, and the successful hunters, rushing up, rescue it from the mauling of their fangs and raise the wild death shout, which is taken up and echoed from a hundred throats.

Hitherto the beaters have had all the fun to themselves, but as the rout moves on a shot is heard in the thick of the bush, and one of our party has given a good account of something. And now we are riding along the brink of a mighty precipice; a rugged peak towers above; beneath, the forest trees rear their heads against the cliff, and the slope falls away into the broad valley. A wilder or more picturesque scene would not easily be found. On all sides the great mountains are sleeping in the golden light of the waning afternoon; far below, the Tugela winds and twists on its serpentine course; but the solemn stillness of Nature on a grand scale is rudely broken in upon, for the whole valley is alive with glistening dark forms flashing through the verdure, and mingling with the baying of their hounds the shouts of the savages are borne on the quiet air.

No bad place for a full view of the hunt is the brow of this same cliff. Extended for about a mile through the bush beneath, a line of Zulus is sweeping on, and we can spy the many-coloured hides of their dogs zig-zagging about in the grass. See, there is a rush towards one spot; a buck is away and the whole pack stringing after him. Spear after spear is hurled, and yet he keeps on; we can still follow his flight and make out his white ' plume.' But he has his work cut out for him before he can clear that fatal circle, for look ! there is another group of dark hunters lying in wait. He sees it too, and literally flies past. Assegais gleam for a moment in a perfect shower, and—the white tuft no longer flits through the bushes. The game little antelope lies on the ground a brown, kicking heap, and the pack comes pouring open-mouthed on to the carcase ; snapping and snarling and tumbling over each other in their eagerness to seize it. Again the loud death-whoop peals through the valley, but before its echoes have died away among the rocks and krantzes, another shout announces the starting of fresh quarry. Thoroughly roused now, only eager for something to slay, they press forward, and the ground is alive with the dark forms of excited savages pouring like ants through the green bush, as some of those high up on the mountain side succeed by a whistle and a yell in slightly turning the buck's course so as to bring him nearer to the party beneath ; but he has a good start and evidently intends to make the most of it. A few assegais are launched at him, but he is out of ' throw ' even for the most powerful and dexterous arm, and they fall harmlessly short. A clamour from the dogs as they rush off on his track, but, blunderheaded brutes, they have been such a long while thinking about it that he can afford to laugh at the lot ; besides, he is unscathed and they haven't a chance. So away he goes, and we can see him ' ricochetting' along, a mere speck, far down there by the river, eluding his fate this time, to meet with it by assegai or bullet in a future ' drive,' or haply to fall a prey to some prowling leopard on the moonlit river-bank in the hush of the still, warm night.

So intent am I watching the progress of the hunt, that I hardly notice a brown shape bounding across an open space at the foot of the cliff, or only take it for one of the Zulu dogs ranging on his own account. It is a buck though, and I only awake to the fact when too late for a shot ; but another of the party, more wary, has delivered the contents of both barrels just as the animal is disappearing among the scrub. Effectively, too, as again that wild shout proclaims, the stricken antelope running blindly into the clutches of a group of beaters. But the afternoon is waning ; it is exceedingly hot, and the natives are beginning to have had enough. We, too, are rather disappointed at the sport not being livelier, for scarce half a dozen shots have been fired by our party, all told. But for my part I am easily consoled with the thought that not for the satisfaction of bringing down the whole ' bag' to my own gun

would I have missed such an opportunity of
watching the affair from beginning to end, and
seeing the natives hunt in their own fashion.

And now it is all over ; the Zulus come strag-
gling up from the valley in long lines, and, gathering on the brow of the cliff, pause for a short rest
before starting homewards. We count head—four
bushbucks and a rock rabbit constitute the spoil ;
might have been worse considering that the day
was somewhat advanced when we began. I suppose I ought to say that I shot something ; the
fact, however, remains unmistakably that I did
not ; indeed I had no opportunity of so much as
letting off my gun, barring the chance just detailed.
But, as before stated, I had a splendid view of
the whole affair.

We ride slowly back ; the natives straggle
across the *veldt*, chattering volubly over the events
of the afternoon. While we are offsaddling at
the store, the weird rhythm of a savage song is
heard, drawing nearer and nearer. The Zulus are
bringing in the spoils of the hunt ; the peculiar
shivering sound of the loose bundles of assegais
which they carry (like no other sound I ever
heard) mingles with the regulated tramp of feet,
and the dark column marches into the open space ;
the perspiration pouring down the glistening hides
of the native hunters, as depositing their weapons

they throw themselves wearily on the ground for a rest.

But they will be lively enough soon, for the cow which has been promised them is even now being driven up to meet her fate. She is young and wild ; so wild, indeed, that none of them quite like going near enough to slay her in their own fashion, and one of our party takes a shot with his rifle, missing a vital part and only wounding her, for the animal is thoroughly frightened, and will not be persuaded to stand still for a single moment ; but the shot starts her off galloping wildly over the plain. With a yell the Zulus dash away in pursuit, forming a wide ring gradually narrowing round the doomed beast, who runs hither and thither. At last, lowering her head, she breaks through the circle with a fierce growling noise, as, shaking her pointed horns and throwing the foam from her mouth, she charges her pursuers, who scatter for a moment, and, closing up again, start swiftly upon her track. At length an assegai flung by a powerful arm buries its sharp blade in her heart, and the poor brute, rolling over and over, expires with a hollow moan. The savages throw themselves on the carcase like a set of vultures, and the work of butchery begins. It is not a pleasant sight though ; moreover, one man, rejoicing in the possession of a knife, perhaps gets on quicker than his fellow who is armed only with an assegai, whereupon they quarrel, and the whole lot are fighting and tearing, gesticulating and screaming—making an unholy and indescribable din; so we leave them to themselves.

Supper over, we proceed to make merry by way of finishing up the undertaking, and the walls of the old shanty ring to the chorus of ' John Peel' and other ditties of world-wide and uproarious fame; and when such of us as are vocalists have exhausted our stock-in-trade and everyone has bawled himself hoarse, some of the natives—who by this have devoured the unfortunate cow, I was going to say even to the skin and horns—are got in and go through their fantastic dance to the accompaniment of a wild war song. The shindy at last becomes deafening, and having had enough of it we eject them; then, rolling ourselves in blankets, turn in beneath the counter of the store —to sleep, if haply we may.

Next morning we return to Sand Spruit, and once more the *veldt* is black with natives who have borne part in the chase and are now on the way home again. An example it behoves me to follow, so taking leave of my brethren of the hunt I inspan and resume the even tenour of my way. Umsinga is left far behind, we cross the Tugela—this time on the pontoon—and wind up the steep rocky

road, to halt on the top of the high ridge overlooking Mooi river. And, next day, as we descend,
my thoughts go back to that hot sunny morning
we toiled up this very bit of road months before,
then starting on a new expedition, every yard in
front *terra incognita*. To-day it seems very much
cognita does that large tract of country over which
I have wandered and am now leaving behind, and
yet I am not half sorry to return to civilisation ;
albeit my trip, with all its ups and downs, has
been far from wearisome and replete with interest
throughout. Crossing the Mooi river we wind
through the wild and beautiful valley, and eventually reach Grey Town, where I part with Andries,
my right hand man, and plod quietly on with the
other two. Then, having covered the forty miles
of road between that place and Maritzburg, I ride
into the capital one fine afternoon, travel-stained
and externally the worse for wear, flannel-shirted
and corduroyed, with countenance fiercely tanned
and blistered by much exposure to the gentle rays
of a South African sun—in short, looking an awful
ruffian—but more thoroughly ' fit' and in ruder
health than ever before in my life.

A week or two to rest and sell off, a run down
to Durban by rail, a few days there, then a bumping
over the ' bar,' and I am once more on board ship—
but, reader, I have not done with you just yet.

CHAPTER XX

Cetywayo at 'Oude Molen'—The King on John Dunn—Former position of Cetywayo—Ncungcwane and the royal attendants—Homeward bound.

LAST, but not least, was my visit to Cetywayo, at the Cape. Armed with a pass from the Secretary for Native Affairs, without which no one is admitted, I took the train out to Mowbray and made my way to 'Oude Molen,' otherwise described as the 'State Prisoners' Location,' where the ex-monarch of Zululand was in durance. About half an hour's walk by a very roundabout way brought me to the place, a building looking as if it might have been a Dutch farmhouse, with stabling and outhouses, but devoid of trees, and standing in the midst of the open flat.

There was no lack of visitors to the ex-King; since the restrictions on seeing him were removed, every day, nearly, one or more parties would arrive at Oude Molen. Having awaited the departure of one of these, I sent in my card to the interpreter, Mr. Dunn, and was admitted. In a front room destitute of furniture but a few chairs, sat the once redoubted potentate, a large, quiet-looking man of between fifty and sixty, dressed in a suit of light tweed, with a yellow embroidered smoking cap on his head. Cetywayo is darker than most Zulus, and has a broad, intelligent face, with good eyes and pleasing expression—on the whole a well-looking man, dignified and courteous in manner, as are nearly all Zulus of rank, and though of large proportions, not corpulent or un-wieldy. The Zulu royal family is proverbial among the nation for stateliness of carriage, and the King is no exception, holding himself very erect, with his head slightly thrown back, as though accustomed to look upon those around him as inferiors.

He shook hands, saying he was glad to see me, but learning that I had just returned from Zulu-land, his face became quite animated over the prospect of hearing about all his old friends and subjects, and through the courtesy of Mr. Dunn, Cetywayo's official interpreter, we were able to have a long chat.

'It was good,' said the King; 'where had I been, and whom had I talked to?'

I began from the very first, and he listened attentively, putting in a remark here and there, and keeping up a running commentary throughout. He seemed intimately acquainted with every foot of the ground I had been over, and would stop me to tell some little anecdote connected with any particular spot, or would give the personal or family history of some one I happened to name. Every now and then his eyes twinkled, and a broad smile would light up his countenance as he related some comic incident regarding the person or persons under discussion. Which goes to show that over and above an intimate acquaintance with his country and people, Cetywayo possesses a strong vein of humour.

At that time the idea of the English visit had been given up, and the unfortunate King was in a state of dire depression. ' Why wouldn't we send him back to his country? He would always be friends with the English.' I ventured to hint at his future policy in the event of restoration; besides, how could we depose the chiefs we had set up in his place? He replied that all Zululand, chiefs and people alike, would hail his return; those who didn't want to live under him could leave the country; he would not punish any of them for having taken part against him hitherto, but if they refused to return to their allegiance, they must leave his country.

I suggested that some of them might be unprepared to acquiesce in so sweeping a change in their fortunes—John Dunn and Sibepu for instance.

'As for John Dunn (he said), he had no following ; a hundred or two of Natal natives. All the Zulus of his clan belonged to him (Cetywayo), also his wives and cattle, and they would all leave John Dunn and come back to him ; but he didn't want *them*. John Dunn might take all his wives and all his cattle and leave the country.' This was hardly a satisfactory answer—evidently the King was not benevolently disposed towards his former ally.

On the subject of his restoration he was very sore. 'Why didn't we allow him to go to England and plead his own cause ? We promised to do so at first and then put him off again. Why should we not send him back to Zululand ? We had taken him away because, we said, he killed his people, and now we had set up chiefs who did far more killing than he (Cetywayo) had ever done. Look at Uhamu, how he had been " eating up " and killing the Abaqulusi. I had been to Hlobane and must know all about it. Did I know how many people Uhamu had killed ? '

I replied that I did not, for certain.

'Eight hundred or a thousand,' said the King.

I expressed incredulity as to it being anything like that number, but he stuck to it—over eight hundred people had been killed by Uhamu ; he (Cetywayo) knew it for certain, and could tell me the actual names of many of the victims. When

I passed Hlobane I could hardly have seen any people about. On this point, however, I was able to set him right, for the kraals in that neighbourhood were all occupied.

Knowing well how a story gains in process of transmission among these people, much after the manner of the proverbial snowball, especially if self-interest leans to the side of exaggeration, I remained unconvinced ; for although, from all accounts, Uhamu had been ' washing his spears ' pretty freely, I don't believe that as a matter of fact his victims were much more than a tenth of the number estimated by Cetywayo.

I had brought with me some photographs of the King's attendants, in which he took great interest, giving me their names and family history, together with those of his women, whom I expressed a wish to see. Accordingly, they having received due notice, I was shown into the next room, where I found the ladies of the royal household, four in number, who, however, did not strike me as being anything out of the common. They were large, tall women, with a hard, not to say sulky, expression, though under the circumstances one could scarcely expect them to look cheerful. Each had her little stock of manufactures spread out on the floor, beadwork, grass spoons, &c., for which, by the way, they demanded full price. I selected a couple of the grass spoons, paying three shillings a piece for the same—I could have got them for a tenth of the value in Zululand, but royalty has its privileges—and rejoicing their hearts with a tin of snuff, I returned to their lord.

Elsewhere in these pages I recorded my conviction that during his exile Cetywayo was about the most popular man in Zululand, and now I thought I quite saw the reason of this popularity. He has a dignified presence, looking every inch a king ; a genial and engaging manner, and now and then his face would be lighted up with a pleasing, good-humoured smile, giving one the impression that he is a man of natural kindliness of heart. That a savage ruler—ay, and a civilised one for that matter—enjoying absolute despotism, should not, under the impulses of sudden passion or undoubted self-interest, be led into the perpetration of occasional acts of cruelty or severity, would be too much to expect of fallen human nature. But what I do say, judging from all I heard and saw, is that Cetywayo is not an ill-dispositioned man, of which, by the way, this fact is not a little significant, that the only one of the Zulu kings who ' died in his bed ' was Mpande, Cetywayo's father and predecessor ; and although for some time previous to that event Cetywayo's power and influence had been steadily increasing, yet he showed no eagerness for his father's death nor made any attempt to accelerate the same. Since his own accession times have become more difficult and dangerous every year, and what with Boer aggression on the one side and Natalian coldness and distrust on the other, it may readily be understood that the position of the Zulu King was not exactly a bed of roses. But that he was animated with a real desire for the welfare of his people and naturally inclined for peace, I have ceased to entertain any doubt. And now, as time goes on and the public at large is beginning to take a dispassionate view of the affair, I believe I am right in saying that an increasing opinion is growing up that he was largely the victim of surrounding circumstances, and that his downfall was not entirely due to his own delinquencies or mistakes. Of one thing I am confident, however ; that many and many a potentate could be found with whom Cetywayo would compare far from unfavourably.

I took leave of the King, who expressed himself glad to have seen me and to have heard all about Zululand and his old friends. Some day perhaps, he said, I should be coming to see him in his own country (a hope that he would eventually be restored kept cropping up throughout his conversation); then he could receive me better, and meanwhile I must be his friend and think well of him.

Passing from the ' royal audience ' I looked in upon the attendants, the principal of whom, Ncungcwane, an elderly man with grizzled hair, is a relation of the King ; most of them being men of rank and fine specimens of their race. Poor fellows, how different they looked, huddling gloomy and taciturn round the fire as the chill evening of a Cape winter day drew in, to the cheerful, lively, good-humoured people I had left in the sunshine and free air on the green hills and plains of Zululand. They brightened up considerably on hearing that I had just been into their old haunts and among their countrymen, and it seemed to me quite like old times standing there, surrounded by the ringed heads and kindly dark faces. But it was too late for much *indaba*, so dividing a canister of snuff amongst the group, I departed and made my way back to the station.

Another twenty-four hours and I am on the deck of the homeward-bound mail steamer, having trodden South African soil for the last time. The steam is up, the shore-bell rings, hurried ' good-byes ' are exchanged, the swarming decks clear by magic of three fourths of their living freight, and amid a cheer from the crowd on the jetty the great ship moves off into the blue waters of Table Bay. We pass Robben Island with its lighthouse ; fainter and indistinct grows the rocky wall of Table Mountain till it fades into the gloom of night, and we stand forth upon our course over the wide ocean—*en route* for Old England.

CHAPTER XXI

Zululand under the Ulundi settlement—Restoration of Cetywayo—
Military system and tactics — Zulu opinion of the Boers—Zulu
character and physique—Religion and superstitions—Formation
and appearance of the country—Climate—Wild animals.

PASSING reference has been made in these pages to a
feeling of unrest prevailing among the Zulus. As a
matter of fact the country at that time, though to all
appearances quiet and peaceful, was not really so ;
for beneath the outward calm lay a strong feeling
of discontent, but one degree removed from open
agitation and actual outbreak.

The results of what is known as the Ulundi
settlement had begun to make themselves felt.
The chiefs set up under that settlement being, with
few exceptions, absolute nobodies, were held in
scant honour, and were practically of but small
power in the land. Of those exceptions Uhamu
had earned the contempt of his countrymen by his
defection from their cause; Hlubi was an alien, and
never had any claim to the allegiance of a single

Zulu ; leaving Tyingwayo, Sibepu, and John Dunn. Powerful *indunas* like Mnyamane, who, by the way, has the reputation of being the shrewdest man in Zululand, were left out in the cold at the time of the settlement of the country, and no notice was taken of any of the King's brothers. Small matter of surprise, then, is it that these worthies, supremely dissatisfied, should sedulously gather round them the disaffected, and hatch plots for the restoration of Cetywayo, with whom had departed their own former glory and *prestige*. Whether there would have been so much outcry for the royal restoration had the country been portioned out between Mnyamane and four or five other influential *indunas* is fair subject for conjecture ; I myself am inclined to think there would not. But under the Ulundi settlement the population soon became divided into two hostile camps, sullenly watching each other with an ill-will they were at no pains to conceal—the Usútu faction, with Mnyamane and Ndabuku, Cetywayo's brother, at its head, on the one hand ; on the other Sibepu, John Dunn, and Uhamu for the maintenance of the Ulundi scheme ; while the remaining chiefs either stood neutral and trimmed between the rival parties, or attached themselves to the one or the other according as self-interest prompted. But the differing interests did more than sit and growl at each other. Sibepu would threaten Ndabuku, and, under colour of a row about some cattle (always a fruitful source of quarrel in Zululand), Mnyamane would make a raid upon Sibepu, who, of course, would retaliate: meanwhile Uhamu amused himself by ' eating up ' a clan of the Abaqulusi in his own territory. The British Resident, having no force at his disposal, could effect little or nothing towards the adjustment of these and other small differences ; and everyone appeared to do pretty much as he chose. All seemed tending, and that not slowly, in the direction of a general blaze.

Then came a lull. A large Zulu deputation started for Maritzburg, and, although it rather ignominiously returned, yet the circumstance of the people having an opportunity of even partially making known their grievance formed, in a measure, a safety-valve. Moreover, the idea of Cetywayo's restoration had been entertained, soon to take tangible shape in his visit to England. Then the ' royalist' chiefs in Zululand knew that the desired restoration was but a question of time, and that nothing would be gained meanwhile by turbulence and rebellion.

And now that the King's rule has been re-established, whether the looked-for result—to wit, the re establishment of peace and contentment—is attained, must depend largely on the policy of the future. That policy it is not within the province of these pages to discuss. Suffice it to say, that Cetywayo himself has no right to be dissatisfied with the terms of his restoration or with the territory allotted to him, the latter being far the greater portion of his former dominion, the whole of which by Zulu law of conquest belongs to us. He could not expect to be put into precisely the same position as before, after the expenditure of blood and treasure we had made in order to remove him from that position, and it must be borne in mind that he was not himself entirely free from blame in the matter of the late war ; wherefore, in all reason, not to say wisdom, he and his people should ' let well alone ' and be thankful.

Formerly looked up to as the despotic head of the most invincible and dreaded of all the native races, Cetywayo has lived to see his rule overthrown, his formidable armies scattered like chaff, and himself carried off to languish in tedious and, to one of his temperament, soul-wearing captivity, only to be emancipated by suing at the very feet of the Power whom in the heyday of his renown he thought to resist. May we not infer that a man of his shrewdness and sagacity will utilise the experience he has gained—in short, will have learnt a lesson.

The military system was set up by Tyaka (or Chaka), under whose influence the Zulus sprung from the small insignificant race they were at the beginning of the present century, into a nation of warriors. They carried on an aggressive warfare with the neighbouring tribes, extending their conquests far and wide : the assegai and the torch were never at rest, and their name became a terror and a scourge. Already was the Zulu army a mighty and formidable engine when Dingane, Tyaka's successor, was brought into collision with the emigrant Boers in 1838. Sanguinary conflicts with the latter, as also the civil war which resulted in the assassination of Dingane and the succession of Mpande (Panda), Cetywayo's father, had somewhat cooled their martial ardour ; and under the rule of this King—a man of mild temper and easy-going habits—a long period of peace ensued, broken only by an occasional raid upon border tribes and the outbreak in 1856 pursuant on the feud between Cetywayo and his brother Umbulazi.

But the army, though unemployed, was not disbanded. Nearly the whole nation was enrolled in regiments according to age, and the military system and tradition remained unbroken. As a matter of fact, enrolment was not compulsory, though one of those *customs* which are stronger than law : it was open to anyone to decline to join the army, but once enlisted, implicit obedience was exacted.   Each regiment had its *induna* and its subalterns, with a commander-in chief over the whole, and there was a wonderful *esprit de corps* throughout: indeed to such an extent did this prevail, that a fight was imminent between any two or more regiments on the occasion of a great national gathering, though all petty differences were sunk in the glory of marching against a common foe.

The tactics employed with such terrible effect against our troops are identical with those of the armies of Tyaka and Dingane ; the outflanking and surrounding, the fierce, resistless, overwhelming rush, and the merciless destruction in the hour of victory of every living thing.   But in one respect the mode of procedure has undergone a change. Tyaka led his warriors in person ; now the *induna* in command posts himself on a hill whence he can overlook the scene of operations, with his staff around him ; for there is a regular staff system consisting mainly of the head *indunas* of each of the various regiments, who, as a rule, are only a kind of ' honorary ' colonel—the sub-chiefs doing all the actual work.   If he sees fit, he despatches one or more of these down to communicate his plans or to effect a rally should there be signs of wavering at any particular point.   In the event of defeat the greater *indunas* lose no time in exemplifying the latter half of an old proverb—in a word, they run away and live to fight another day, or rather to see that their subordinates fight. But although the martial spirit is still alive in Zululand—every man will tell you with some pride to what regiment he belongs—cohesion has been completely destroyed by the many differing and rival interests which have cropped up within the last three years, and to re-organise the army on the old lines would be to-day next to an impossibility. I say to-day, because, as before stated, the events of the future must depend on the policy of the future.

One fine quality which the Zulus possess is a readiness to forgive and forget. They bear no malice, and, considering that, whether rightly or wrongly, we invaded their country, slaughtered thousands of their best warriors, burnt their kraals, carried off their king, and reduced them— the most powerful nation in Southern Africa—to the condition of a conquered race, it is surprising how little resentment is entertained towards us. They say it was all the ' fortune of war,' ' it is past, and there's an end of it,' and they welcome the Englishman wherever he goes with the same cheerful and hearty greeting.

But this goodwill in no wise extends to their Transvaal neighbours, whom they hold in abhorrence. The very mention of the Boers would evoke strong expressions of contempt and detestation, and when pressed for a reason it was everywhere the same story. ' They are mean, and liars—always on the look-out to steal our land.' One chief told me he would like nothing better than to be allowed to lead an *impi* against the *Amabuna* (Boers). ' But,' I objected, just to see what he would say, ' don't you know that they defeated *us* at Majuba ? '

' Yes,' was the reply, ' but the English could have eaten them up afterwards if they had chosen. *We* defeated the English at Isandhlwana, but where are we now ? So it would have been with the *Amabuna*.'

This was looking at the affair in its proper light, which I found the Zulus did as a rule; not being at all inclined to rate Dutch prowess any higher because it had proved too much for us under certain circumstances.

The Zulu character has been greatly misrepresented. We have been accustomed to look upon this unfortunate nation as a horde of fierce untameable barbarians whose every thought is of war; rapine and massacre its *summum bonum* of existence, and among whom the most ordinary virtues are unknown—and upon its king as a tyrannical despot and a monster of cruelty. Instead, what do we find? A quiet, kindly, lighthearted race ; sober, cleanly, and honest—loyally attached, too, to its exiled King, supposed to be such a detestable tyrant. It would be idle, of course, not to expect occasional turbulence and disquietude among a brave, warlike people with great military traditions, but I maintain that the Zulu is by nature of a quiet and kindly disposition, not wanting in generosity, and good-humoured to a degree; in short, far from being a mere brutal savage. He has his faults indeed, and if merciless and cruel in the madness and exultation of victory, at any rate it is the blind ferocity of the wild beast whose rage is satiated with the death of an enemy, not the refined barbarity of the Red Indian or the Oriental delighting in the prolonged torments of his victim.

The physique of the Zulus has been much ex-aggerated. They are by no means the brawny athletes of popular notion and illustrated periodi-cal, it being, in fact, the rarest thing to find a man with any extraordinary development of biceps; as a rule they are smooth-limbed rather than other-wise, though tall and well built. But they make up for muscular deficiency by a wonderful supple-ness and agility, being lithe and active as wild cats, and with a hardihood and constitution of iron. And they are fine-looking—in many instances handsome—men, with erect, graceful carriage and considerable dignity of aspect. You never, for instance, see a Zulu with head sunk on his chest, or bandy-legged, or with a stoop in the shoulders. As adversaries, man for man they are not more formidable than any other race ; it is the moral effect—on themselves no less than on their enemies —of the trained and disciplined regiments, the honour and glory of which, in a measure, each man feels to be centred in himself; the mighty army in all its savage panoply, and the great traditions at its back—this is what renders the Zulu attack so terrific and irresistible.

As regards religion the Zulus may be said to hold no definite belief whatever. They have no temples, no idols or gods of any kind, no priests or altars, and no recognised or national cult. They have a hazy belief in a Supreme Being whom they call 'Nkulu'nkulu,' ' the Great Great One,' and a vague tradition about creation ; otherwise they are given to superstition of various kinds. You never meet a single Zulu abroad at night, very rarely any at all ; if forced then to travel they go in a body. What they are afraid of they hardly know ; goblins are supposed to be disporting themselves whom it is well not to meet ; wherefore they do their journeying by day. I had a considerable amount of night travelling, but not one instance can I recollect of meeting a Zulu on the road an hour after dark. Nor would they stay, if talking to me at sundown, unless their kraal was very near indeed, and only then if it was a bright moonlight evening.

They are great believers in witchcraft and the power of the evil eye. If any one is seized with an illness at all out of the common, it is *tagati* (witchcraft), and the *izanusi* (doctors) perform their incantations over the hapless patient by way of exorcising the evil spirit; for which ' professional attendance' the rascals take care that they are well remunerated. In the event of a chief or man of rank being afflicted, a 'smelling out' takes place, and after much ceremonial, which has been too often described to need reiteration here, the soothsayers, singling out some obnoxious person, denounce him as the offender; whereupon his cattle and goods are confiscated, and he and his family are fortunate if allowed to escape with their lives. That tyrannical quackery of this kind should be thus deeply rooted in the minds of a people otherwise so shrewd is simply amazing. They firmly believed in the inspiration of the *izanusi*, and although no man knew but what his turn would come next, yet they all acquiesced in the practice of 'smelling out' as a national institution wherein nothing could shake their faith.

Signs and omens play an important part in

their scheme. Phenomena in the heavens, unusual meteorological occurrences, the flight of a particular bird, and a hundred other trifles constitute omens of greater or less importance, to explain which the ' spirits' must be consulted and sacrifices —generally of cattle—offered upon the graves of departed chiefs. Of a future state they have little if any idea, and, as before mentioned, they have a vague belief in the Deity, but of definite religion or recognised cult the Zulus have none.

The formation of the country is capricious in the extreme ; elevated and smooth table-lands suddenly alternating with broad valleys and lofty mountains, and where least expected yawn deep rifts. It is not a well wooded region on the whole. Bush abounds in more or less profusion in the basins formed by the valleys of the greater rivers and in the tropical heat of the low-lying coast lands, but the larger portion of the country is open and treeless. A fine pasture land and well watered, but the broad plains and rounded slopes, waving with tall luxuriant grass, seem rather fitted for grazing than for purposes of cultivation.

What may be the hidden resources of the country I can only conjecture. Coal is talked of, and I did happen to hear significant hints about gold being found in such and such a place ; as to its existence I have no doubt, whether in quantities sufficient to prove remunerative is another thing. Some of the rivers have every appearance of being auriferous, notably the Ityotyozi, which flows over a fine sandy bed, through an alluvial soil studded with quartz. A prospecting party visited this river about a year after the war, but the results not being encouraging the undertaking was abandoned.

In the matter of climate, though warm in summer, it is far from unhealthy, and the nights are delicious. In the low-lying coast country the heat is great, and has all the damp, enervating feeling of tropical latitudes, to which may be due the circumstance of the natives on the high open ' steppes ' of northern and western Zululand being far superior in physique and character to their brethren of the coast. The winter months, May, June, and July, are exceedingly cold ; keen, biting winds sweep across the treeless wastes, and snow and sleet are of no infrequent occurrence.

Of wild animals and birds the greater variety is met with in the bush country. The rhebok and stembok are to be shot on the open undulating plains, which also abound in quail, with here and there a sprinkling of partridges. The pauw and the koorhaan—both ' leery ' birds—whom you may stalk at early morn in the long soaking grass till wet to the skin, but not by a foot can you diminish that reprehensible fifty yards which is to bring you

within range, and your quarry, tired at length of
dragging you through the penetrating dew, heaves
up its great carcase and flaps off with a peevish
yell. The crane, with his blue slaty plumage, stalks
solemnly about ; and the plover circles overhead
in the gloaming, sounding his shrill pipe.   Spreuws
whistle among the krantzes, the dainty sugar-bird [1]
dips his long needle-like bill into the red tubes of
the aloe blossoms, and the reed beds and bushes
overhanging river or water-hole are alive with the
twittering of clouds of yellow ' finks ' whose pendu-
lous nests sway and dip in the breeze. Birds of
prey, too, from the huge cinereous vulture and the
crested eagle to the little red kestrel, soar above
the waste.

The bark of the bushbuck echoes through
black, wooded ravines among whose caves and
frowning krantzes the savage leopard makes his
home ; monkeys skip amid the gnarled boughs of
the yellow-wood trees ; jackals share the ground
burrows with the ant bear and the porcupine, and
the large striped hyæna howls along the river bank
in the moonlight. The dark forests of Ingome
still afford cover to the beautiful koodoo with his
long spiral horns, and their wild recesses are not
guiltless of lions. Northward the lonely lagoons
around San Lucia Bay resound with the splash

[1] A species of humming bird.

and snort of the hippopotamus, and in the reed-fringed pools and quiet depths of the larger rivers dwell the crocodile and iguana. Of serpents, the cobra, the puff adder, and the mamba are the most dangerous, but except in certain localities are not common enough to constitute any real source of peril.

Hardly a land that one would visit in quest of sport—albeit with dogs and appliances a keen sportsman who laid himself out therefor would not do badly in this line—to the traveller it is full of interest. The inhabitants are an intelligent and kindly disposed race; above all, the climate is healthy, and anybody desiring a complete change and a few months of life in the open air, might do worse than follow my example and go 'Through the Zulu Country.'